Copyright © 2016 by Betsy Chasse
All rights reserved. No part of this publication may be reproduced, distributed, or transmitted in any form or by any means, including photocopying, recording, or other electronic or mechanical methods, without the prior written permission of the publisher, except in the case of brief quotations embodied in critical reviews and certain other noncommercial uses permitted by copyright law. For permission requests, write to the publisher, addressed "Attention: Permissions Coordinator," at the address below.
BC Movie, LLC
PO Box 4985 Chatsworth, CA 91311
www.betsychasse.net
Printed in the United States of America

ISBN: 978-1-68418-976-2

CONTENTS

CHAPTER 1 — 2

THE ORIGIN OF COACHING...NECESSITY IS THE MOTHER OF EACH NEW PROFESSION!
Chérie Carter-Scott, Ph.D. MCC

CHAPTER 2 — 14

LIVING LIFE AS A COACH
Lynn U Stewart, PCC

CHAPTER 3 — 22

THE #1 SECRET OF BUILDING A MILLION DOLLAR COACHING PRACTICE
David Steele, MA, MFT, CPC

CHAPTER 4 — 32

BRING YOUR WHOLE SELF TO WORK: USING INTEGRAL INTELLIGENCE® TO THRIVE AS A COACH AND CREATE A SUSTAINABLE COACHING PRACTICE
Donna Stoneham, Ph.D.

CHAPTER 5 — 46

NATURAL COURAGE: CREATING A BUSINESS WITH CLARITY, CREATIVITY, AND CHOICE
Carol Koziol, MA, PCC

CHAPTER 6 — 54

FIVE CRITICAL MISTAKES TO AVOID WHEN BUILDING A COACHING NICHE
Sayeda Habib, PCC

CHAPTER 7   64

MARKETING YOUR COACHING SERVICES TO LOCAL COLLEGES AND UNIVERSITIES
Wendy L. Yost

CHAPTER 8   78

A TRULY SUCCESSFUL AND SUSTAINABLE BUSINESS MODEL FOR COACHES.
Tim Johnson

CHAPTER 9   90

IT'S ABOUT PEOPLE NOT PROCESS
Dr. Jane Cox

CHAPTER 10   100

THE YES CODE
Carol Look, LCSW, Creator of The Yes Code

CHAPTER 11   112

TIPS FOR AUTHENTIC COACHING SUCCESS
Kristin Grayce McGary

CHAPTER 12   122

BE THAT 'SOMEONE'...
"WHAT WE REALLY NEED IS SOMEONE WHO CAN BRING OUT THE BEST IN US."
Thomas Gelmi

CHAPTER 13   132

MASTERING CROSS-CULTURAL COACHING ABROAD EXECUTIVE & LIFE COACHING ON THE ROAD!
Michael A. Pomije, PCC

CHAPTER 14   144

SOCIAL MEDIA SHAPES & FORMS THE WORLD
Kate Gardner

CHAPTER 15   154

"LAW OF ATTRACTION" COACHING
Christy Whitman

CHAPTER 16   160

POWER FROM PAIN
Jami and Marla Keller

CHAPTER 17   168

3E - EVOKE, EMBRACE, EVOLVE
Liza Boubari, CCHt, CSMc

Betsy Chasse is an award winning filmmaker and Best selling Author most notable for "What The Bleep Do We Know" and her book "Tipping Sacred Cows"
www.betsychasse.net

FOREWORD
Betsy Chasse

I had the opportunity to spend almost a year with these Coaches, learning about their craft, their business and why they became Coaches and it inspired me. I have met many who called themselves coaches who had nothing more than a weekend course under their belt. Don't get me wrong, there are many amazing weekend courses on coaching. One should always expand their minds. However, with the Coaches in this book, it's more than just a weekend course or something they added to their repertoire. It's their career. They have spent years studying, building, ever exploring the science behind what they do. Becoming experts at understanding the Human Condition and then providing the Code to their clients on moving through life's challenges.

As a filmmaker and author, I get to have fun in this world of helping people, without really any responsibility. Although I take what I do very seriously. What I learned from these amazing people, is that when you say you're a Coach you have a responsibility, to not only understand what that means, as in Coaching isn't therapy, Coaching isn't self-help. Coaching is an amazing tool given to someone who is ready and willing to take the next step in their lives or their careers and it requires more than just an MBA, it requires more than just the experience. It takes a certain type of person to be a coach, willing to allow their client to explore their own hearts and mind. A Coach is talented guide committed to your success while also committed to assisting you in finding it. A Coach isn't there to give you the answers, a gifted coach knows how to truly assist you in finding it for yourself.

If you have a calling to be a Coach, you made the right choice in reading this book. They might not be "Big, Famous" names, they haven't cared to be. These Coaches are the real deal. Successful, sustainable practices that span decades.

The tips given aren't quick fixes, or get rich quick schemes, there are a plethora of those on Facebook. What you're going to get is practical advice on how to build your own career. One that spans your lifetime, one that fulfils not only your bank account, but your heart.

1 | Chérie Carter-Scott, Ph.D. MCC

Dr. Chérie Carter-Scott, MCC from International Coach Federation with over 10,000 hours; she is the original Life Coach and founder of the Coaching Industry. Dr. Chérie is a Master Coach who trains people to become executive and/or life coaches through MMS Institute, LLC (USA), MMSWI, BV (NL) and Motivation Coaching Service, Ltd (Bangkok, TH). To learn more about Dr. Chérie's coach trainings, go to their websites: http://www.motherofcoaching.com/, www.drcherie.com, www.themms.com, www.themms.eu, www.mmsvt.com, and www.negaholics.com. They can also be reached by phone (800) 321-6342 or contact info@themms.com for more information about MMS Coach Training.

CHAPTER 1

THE ORIGIN OF COACHING... NECESSITY IS THE MOTHER OF EACH NEW PROFESSION!

Chérie Carter-Scott, Ph.D. MCC
The Mother of Coaching

In 1974 I was searching my mind, heart, and soul for the purpose of my life, when a colleague asked me if I could help him sort out some issues regarding his company. My experience was limited when it came to business matters, and I couldn't imagine what value I would bring to his situation. I declined his invitation and continued my quest for meaning and relevance. He called two additional times and asked if I could help him. Becoming mildly irritated at his insistence, I asked him, "Why are you calling me?" To which he replied, "Because I trust you." I protested, "But I don't know anything." He retorted, "That could be very helpful!" Dismayed, I stated, "If you completely understand that I know nothing about your business, and you are willing to pay me to help you sort out the issues, then I accept!"

In October 1974, we started the project and Lloyd became my first official coaching client. After a successful coaching assignment, he started sharing his amazing results with everyone he came in contact with... his comments sounded like, "Chérie asked me incredibly powerful questions. Not sure what to call it, but what she did was very effective." My phone started to ring off the hook. Before I knew it I was coaching people everyday, and the referrals kept coming. I continued to protest saying, "I don't know anything... however, I will ask you questions and you will discover your own answers." The people who called didn't care that I wasn't a Ph.D., an MBA, or a psychologist since the enthusiasm regarding the coaching sessions were so positive. There was only one thing that I was absolutely certain of… I really didn't know answers, guidance, or advice for anyone. In short, I knew that I didn't know… much…about anything! That perceived liability actually turned into my greatest asset.

Within three months, clients began asking if I could teach them how to do what I did. They wanted to have the same skills that I was utilizing with my clients. They wanted to be able to ask powerful, penetrating, profound, life-altering questions to help their clients, patients, and customers discover their own answers. Since I was perceived as an unconscious competent—one who is totally unaware of the impact of her efforts— I didn't know if I could figure out what I was doing that was perceived as so impactful. I knew I helped my clients focus, determine what they wanted, and make clear choices, however, I had no idea how the combination of intention, skills, abilities, and the use of my energy could create such extraordinary results. People used the word, "Gifted" to describe what I did, but like a prodigy, empowering people came so naturally to me, without effort or performance anxiety, that I dismissed the impact of the sessions I was conducting.

With the help of my friend, Kathy, we started to examine and analyze what I was doing that was making such a profound difference. The most important aspect was that I was fundamentally certain that I didn't know the answers for anyone. I also believed that each person possessed their own answers to all of their challenges, and I never presumed to know for anyone else what their choices or actions should be. This was the perfect starting place, and from there Kathy assessed everything I did with clients that was effective. The initial behaviors were obvious and she immediately noticed that I easily suspended judgment—something Kathy said was not so easy for everyone to do. I didn't know that setting aside judgments was so challenging for others; we therefore set out to find the root of judgmental behavior in order to unlock that mechanism.

I thought, "If I can suspend judgment, it must be possible for others to do as well!" We needed to determine, however, how to unlock this almost knee-jerk reaction in the judgmental mechanism. In addition to suspending judgment, we had to find a way to train people to not know the answers and stop giving advice to others. Since providing advice was an automatic reaction, trained over time, in numerous years of formal educational, we believed that it would take a concerted effort to reverse this behavior. We thought that if an individual exhumed their own dreams, they might experience the visioning process from the inside out and be more sensitive to the fragility of the human psyche and emotions. In other words, if they experienced the process of recalling, honoring, and treasuring their precious dreams, they would be more respectful of the dreams, wishes, and goals of others.

We further determined that actively listening to the client was essential to the coaching process, but the question remained, "how could you listen to another if your mind was actively chattering at you?" We needed to find ways to help people silence the voices of their mind, at least temporarily, for at least an hour, so that the coach could listen intently and focus on what was being said, and what was not said. This focus of attention was critically important. We queried, "How could we shift their attention off of themselves and 100% onto the other person?" This was another challenge that we were addressing.

My two colleagues, Kathy and Carol, noticed these powerful questions that seemed to be plucked out of thin air. When Kathy asked me where those questions came from, I said that I listened closely to the client's answers, and the next question became obvious. If I were paying close attention to what was stated, the "Clue" would surface and reveal itself to me. If my mind were elsewhere, I would definitely miss it.

As we proceeded with the analysis of my behaviors that created a safe coaching environment, more elements started to surface. Kathy and Carol noticed that I used the techniques of restating the objective and subsequently recapping at strategic moments. I was unaware of this tendency, however I acknowledged that I sincerely wanted to ensure that I understood what was being communicated to me; I also wanted to confirm that we were in synch as we progressed in this partnership. Although I didn't want to be irritating to the client, I really wanted to ensure that I hadn't missed something, assumed, or lost the thread of the client's communication.

Kathy commented that I never once gave advice; I shared with her that since I knew nothing about the client's situation, it would have been presumptuous or even arrogant of me to imagine that I had any advice that might be remotely helpful. I commented, "Listening closely in a non-judgmental manner, reflecting back what I heard, asking questions that go deeper, and being very respectful of the client's inner wishes, dreams, goals, and fears enabled me to help them find their inner GPS guiding them through their challenges to their goals." Kathy was very respectful when she requested to observe a session with a client; she closely watched what I did to determine whatever I did that I was unaware of. We obtained permission from a client for Kathy to be present and she observed quietly in the corner, clipboard in hand.

After the session, Kathy commented, "I have a whole new list of behaviors that I just observed." She continued to list my coaching behaviors, the behaviors of the "Unconscious Competent." Kathy noticed, "You were sincerely curious and interested in your client and their challenge, and you asked several times about their feelings regarding related items. You were connected to the client and when that connection became shaky you took responsibility to repair the disconnection. There was an interesting blend of caring coupled with empowerment. You weren't weak or mushy, nor were you pushy or forceful. You didn't get shaken when feelings surfaced, which was impressive, and although empathetic, you didn't take on their feelings or get enmeshed in them. How did you do that?" she queried.

Kathy continued to list the many behaviors that I demonstrated, and eventually we had a rather extensive list. This was the first step in the process. Carol helped me design the first MMS Coach Training in 1974 based on the core competencies observed by Kathy. Carol was the ideal associate because she was collaborative, curious, enthusiastic, eager, and non-judgmental. With Kathy's list in hand…we set out to design the MMS Coach Training, the method that would teach people to coach their clients, patients, and customers in the same way I was coaching them. Our initial list of behaviors are listed here:

- Coach connected with client (synching mind, body, and spirit)
- Clarified time and outcome expectations
- Established a clear achievable objective
- Was sincerely interested
- Understood the client's objective
- Was non-judgmental throughout

The Coach

- Asked about related feelings
- Restated information naturally
- Focused attention on client
- Actively listened
- Was in flow
- Did what was necessary to stay in flow
- Acknowledged when out of flow
- Coach took care of him/herself
- Asked clear and open-ended questions
- Used "clues" to create questions
- Believed in the client's ability
- Was unattached to the outcome
- Took the client into fantasy or ideal outcome
- Recapped at strategic moments
- Acknowledged when confused or stuck
- "Chauffeured" session effortlessly
- Supported rather than directed
- Maintained objectivity
- Used client's choice of words
- Used heart and power chakras
- Closed sexual and third eye chakras
- Acknowledged mirrors when helpful
- The client made a choice
- It felt complete to both people
- The "WOW" factor illuminated the client
- Brought the session to closure

We came up with the following core values that we wanted to be woven throughout the fabric of our MMS Coach Training. Those values were:

- Acceptance
- Awareness
- Balance
- Causality
- Clarity
- Creativity
- Completion
- Empowerment
- Encouragement

- Fairness
- Feedback
- Gratitude
- Inspiration
- Intention
- Letting go
- Listening
- Setting Objectives
- Support
- Trust

It became clear that the design of the training needed to address both cognitive and affective aspects of the participants; it also needed to include content and process, emphasizing behavior changes as well as learning new skills and techniques. We were also defining a new profession for individuals to consider, one that hadn't yet been invented. We needed to package it in such a way that didactic, and experiential learning could all be interwoven into each module incorporating different learning styles so that all students could have their needs accommodated. If a person was more cognitive, we needed to accommodate that learning style. If a person was more experiential, we needed to ensure that their needs would be attended to. Since some people are auditory, we wanted to ensure that our resources were supplied in auditory format as well. We didn't want to exclude anyone. In addition, we wanted each group to be cohesive, supportive, and conducive to the learning environment. The blend of structure, and freedom was an important balance. The core competencies needed to be in place, and we wanted our MMS coaches to be their authentic selves, not clones or imitations of me.

Professions come into existence when there is a need; they die out when that need has been replaced with a new invention, an improved process, an innovative technology that causes the old profession to become obsolete. As the coaching profession grew, I trained more and more people, MMS continued to expand conducting trainings across the globe. In our fast-paced, intense, and ever-changing world, coaching helps unearth vision and passion, focus motivation, develop gravitas, and facilitate successful transitions.

Why corporations and individuals seek out a professional coach…

- To sort out options and determine the most preferable direction
- To uncover one's underlying preference and receive support
- To manage the gap between where you are presently and your desired future
- To assist in overcoming obstacles and breaking through blocks
- To support in the achievement of career goals
- To help articulate capabilities, direction, new visions, vistas, and ventures
- To help process disappointment, dismissal, or disillusionment
- To develop self-confidence and to learn to believe in oneself

To find the building blocks between your current perception of yourself and the desired future identity (eg. Manager to leader)

To build needed skills to provide upward mobility, i.e. "gravitas"

Corporations Want Coaches for a Variety of Reasons...
- To enhance performance
- To increase effectiveness on the job
- To help executives develop "People-soft skills"
- To augment gaps in their professional development
- To prepare them for increasing demands with additional "Promote-ability"
- To develop a variety of skills in preparation for leadership
- To help executives become more self-confident and able to receive feedback

To become smarter with time and task management

Types of Situations That Are Coachable
- To assist cultural integration in M&A
- To eliminate gaps between the present and the transitional future
- To breakthrough obstacles like in the film, "The King's Speech"
- To address confidential and sensitive situations
- To support relocation orientation support
- To assist transitions between assignments or careers
- To formulate visions, goals, and strategies
- To overcome challenges with personalities on the job (or off)
- To facilitate choice-making from an inner-directed place

NOTE: It is less expensive to hire a coach to support an existing executive, than to replace that valuable resource with a new one.

The expansion of the coaching profession
In 1995 Coach Thomas Leonard started International Coach Federation (ICF) as a nonprofit organization for fellow coaches to support each other and grow the coaching profession. The aggressive growth of ICF has helped legitimize the coaching profession. According to the ICF 2014 Global Coaching Study, approximately 50,000 professional coaches are now in business worldwide as compared to 2,100 professional coaches in 1999. In 2016, ICF is located in over 100 countries, and is currently adding a staggering 2,000 new members each year.

ICF is a professional coaching community that promotes credibility for the coaching profession. ICF clarifies expectations for coaches and clients, certifies coaches and accredits organizations. ICF has established ethical guidelines for both coaches and clients, with agreed upon standardized "Core Competencies" for all ICF coaches.

Some of the benefits of ICF are:
- A larger community of coaches
- Builds credibility
- Code of Ethics that rules the industry
- Common frame of references
- Common language
- Conferences to attend when you are a member
- Keeps your coaching crisp and your skills current
- Standardization of competencies

ICF defines coaching as partnering with clients in a thought-provoking and creative process that inspires them to maximize their personal and professional potential, which is deliberately broad and is designed to encompass many varied approaches. The ICF has stipulated Core Competencies to standardize the practice of coaching in order to increase the professionalism in the industry. Coaching has proved to be a valuable tool and when you are sensitive to the culture, the results can be absolutely profound.

Since our organization pre-dates ICF by 21 years, initially we didn't perceive the value it would add to the overall coaching community. Remember, in the year 1974, only Dr. Chérie and MMS were teaching people how to coach. Since we started in the US, expanded to Europe in 1988, and then to Asia in 2010, we found that we needed to incorporate cultural differences into our coaching. In some instances, the differences were linguistic. For example, turnover in the US means staff turnover and is not a positive term; in Europe, turnover relates to profits and is extremely positive. In other cases the cultural differences were behavioral. Where Americans are generally enthusiastic and self-promotional, Europeans were more subdued, restrained, and self-diminishing. We had to adapt our style to the more thoughtful and methodical approach of Northern Europe in order for coaching to take hold. Our first MMS Coach Training in Europe was conducted in Holland in 1990. In 2013, we were conducting entrepreneurial trainings in India. When the subject of pre-arranged marriages was presented as the norm, we initially had a typically Western reaction. When we probed a little deeper we discovered a very hierarchical and paternalistic culture where children were expected to please their parents with their various life choices. We seriously wondered if coaching would ever catch on in India given their outer-centered cultural penchant. Three years later, India happens to be one of the fastest growing coaching countries in the world!

One of the main focuses of our international coaching has been to bridge gaps between diverse cultures. As foreigners in many new locations, we rapidly became students of the customs, the languages, and the cultures. The more we learned, the hungrier we became to understand the subtleties and nuances that we hadn't been briefed on and didn't quite understand specifically pertaining to culture. It is important to define what we mean when we use the word, "Culture."

Defining Culture
Culture is the collection of values, learned beliefs, and behavioral dictates that are shared within a group of people that is self-sustaining and transfers these paradigms from generation to generation. Culture is typically defined as, ways of living, behavioral norms and expectations, language and linguistic expressions, styles of communication, patterns of thinking, beliefs, and values of a particular group. A culture may include shared language, folklore, ideas, thinking patterns, concepts held in common, communication styles, and accepted "truths" held sacred by members of the group. In addition, members of a culture have similar expectations of life itself. Culture serves as a road map for both perceiving and interacting with the world. Another way we can define culture is to say that culture is the behavioral software that programs us

to conform to the expectations of the larger group.

Frequently, culture plays a greater role in determining communication behavior than race, ethnicity, or other diversity factors and can be what creates conflicts because of differences in perception, orientation, beliefs, and communication styles associated with those cultures. Some facts are:
· Culture determines attitudes and behaviors
· Most cultural norms and rules are assumed and not formally written down
· People's behaviors are interpreted through each person's cultural filter
· No human being is "culture-exempt"

Numerous opportunities have been presented to us to coach in multinational companies, at all levels of the organization, to support individuals, teams, and departments in exceeding expectations and causing extraordinary results. Our international expansion has provided us with the opportunity to coach and train coaches in Holland, Hong Kong, Hungary, Singapore, Sweden, Switzerland, Germany, Thailand, China, India, US, Ethiopia, and Vietnam. Each group of people has taught us lessons, and we have been humbled by the experience of learning about diverse cultures.

I am passionate about coaching and see applications for this incredibly powerful tool everywhere. Teaching coaches worldwide became the purpose of my life, and I feel blessed and honored to be doing this incredible work.

Lynn U Stewart, PCC

Lynn U Stewart, PCC. After an adventurous life with careers in education and hotel managment Lynn became the first MMS certified coach trained personally by Dr. Chérie Carter-Scott. In 1979 she went on to lead the MMS organization as its President and CEO. In 1981, she opened the first remote office in Aspen Colorado. She assisted in training coaches across the US then expanded the organization globally by moving to Amsterdam, Holland. She lives there today as Director of The MMS Worldwide Institute.

The MMS Worldwide Institute became accredited by the (ICF) International Coach Federation in 2013 and presents both the ACTP and the ACSTH. Because of their ethical guidelines, MMS believed that ICF would bring a new level of professionalism to their clients, graduates, and students as well as to the coaching industry.

Lynn@themms.com
http://www.themmsinstitute.com

CHAPTER 2

LIVING LIFE AS A COACH

Lynn U Stewart, PCC

These twelve steps sum up what it means to live the life of a brilliant transformational life coach. You listen to your own inner wisdom and go where the guidance, messages, and lessons take you. When you live according to the coaching principles you don't necessarily fit into the world of convention, but rather connect with your own purpose and align yourself with your value system and principles. When you live the process you are committed to fulfillment rather than the trappings of success. You are dedicated to authenticity rather than position, prestige, or perks. You are devoted to the truth and honoring your ultimate purpose in life rather than momentary appetite gratification. It is because you have this unswerving allegiance to connection, meaning and the deeper values in life that you have the ability to support your clients, colleagues and friends in being loyal to their higher selves. When you live the process, you encourage, empower, and enkindle joy in others aligning them with their true essence and values.

Read the Twelve Steps to Living the Process and ask yourself if you are willing to live life from this joyful orientation.

1) Enjoy every day of your life and to have fun doing whatever you do. Joy is not so much found in any particular action since it is generated by the person who is performing the act. When you find the joy within you, you bring it with you wherever you go to whatever activity you choose. Roland finds joy and excitement in everything he does. When he goes for a walk he looks for interesting stops on the route. When he schedules an evening at home he creates a gourmet meal shopping in markets that please him. When he looks at free afternoon, he gives himself and others three options that are all fun: museum, movie, or art gallery. He is always

looking for ways to enhance his days with well-planned small events. He calls these outings "the small vacation."

2) Feel, experience and honor your feelings. Feelings are the outward expression of your innermost reality. Feelings enable you to connect with your authentic self. Emotions connect your physical self with your spirit self and are a barometer of your overall well-being. Your feelings indicate how you are in relationship to yourself and others. When you allow your feelings you show that you respect your reality. When you honor your feelings you place your personal experience above saving face or pleasing others.

Carolyn is a hard working executive with a demanding home life. With three teenagers and a corporate husband she must stay close to her feelings in order to stay on top of all of their demands. In a session, she discovered that she has a truth detector inside that says both "stop" and "No" to which she rarely listens. Her take away from our session was to exercise the "No" muscle and claim her space when she gets the "Message." She created a fire drill. Whenever overwhelm sets in, listen intently to the signals which usually sound like little stress warnings. She admitted to having a slight ringing in her ears when things get out of balance. When the fun goes away, she tunes out. She now sees the warning signals. She feels certain that she will respond accordingly and get back on track.

3) Tell the truth, your truth to the best of your ability. Telling the truth means that you look deeper than the surface explanation or your immediate circumstances. Telling the truth means that you go beyond appropriateness and decorum and reveal what is sometimes unspeakable. Telling the truth is about being your authentic self and letting others experience it, regardless of their reaction.

Margaret from Switzerland was having trouble finding her ability to speak out and say the unspeakable. Born to be a Swiss wife and mother, she felt that her job was to take care of the family needs. "Yes" was her normal response to all requests. She seldom put herself first. When she realized this, she found that her truth was often unacceptable. In the Inner Negotiation Workshop, a two-day experience, she realized that the hardest people with whom to be honest were her husband and her son.

She felt it was her duty to do whatever her husband/family asked. In the safe and supportive workshop environment, she asked a man to act the part of her husband and ask her if she would take his shoes to the shoe repair shop. Everything inside was saying "No" yet what came out of her mouth was a familiar "Yes dear." The Yes was so engrained that she asked me if there were a short circuit between her knowing and her mouth since she could not say "No." After several go-rounds she finally was able to find her "No" but not without a struggle. Throughout the rest of the workshop she asked various participants to ask her to do things …so she could refuse… immediately! Her buried level of truth was restored. She rediscovered her truth in the two-day intensive.

4) Look within yourself for your messages, guidance, and direction… when you discover it, trust it, honor it and follow it. Looking within means that you are devoted to the spiritual side of your nature. It means that you reflect on your options and choices before you act, checking in with your essence. Messages, guidance and direction are always there if you are willing to take the time to listen and notice what they are telling you.

Richard, an IT professional, was constantly being bypassed in his job. He came to the workshop to find out why. A mild mannered kind man, 2 meters tall Richard had no idea what to do. All of a sudden out of no where he got the message to roar, like a lion. Feeling embarrassed and shy he told the group about his strange message. After fighting with the strange inner request he asked the group if anyone would mind if he enacted his message. Delighted with the thought of Richard having to roar, the supportive participants gave him the green light. He jumped from his chair, in a crouched position, he began to roar at his fellow participants. He successfully enacted his new found lion-hood. He roared around the room twice and finally created a standing ovation. As he returned to his chair his body was vibrating. When asked about his shaking he said he felt like a computer whose reset button had just been pushed. Upon reflection he felt like a small boy who had been constantly disappointed by his father's absence at key moments in his childhood. With no words to express, Richard was powerless. Additionally, as an adult, his father was two hours late for his wedding. The lion within opened the door to promotions and validation from his employer. Richard was chosen and acknowledged for his IT wizardry with a promotion and a raise.

5) Focus on solutions rather than on problems. You have two options: either dwell on the problem or on the solution. It is always your choice, however, the problem gives headaches and heartaches and the solution provides a wonderful lightness of being. When you are committed to the solution, it means that you won't allow the problem to slow you down, drag you down, or sour your spirit. It means that you always know that there is a solution to every problem and you strive to create win-win outcomes.

Alycia had sold her business and was elated knowing that she could join the dream company as a free lancer. Two women had brought her business and the hand off day had arrived for the transfer. The celebration party was that afternoon. The first stop that morning, was the monogram store where she had bought books for the new owners. The books were not ready. Not to be put off by the delay, she had just enough time to get to the nail salon. After getting her nails manicured, she made her way to the counter where she paid her check only to realize she had smudged three of her nails while retrieving her keys. Not to be daunted by the series of events, she bought the matching bottle of nail polish and got into her car where she repaired the damage.
On the way out of the parking garage she heard a familiar thump, thump, thump as the car limped toward the cashier. A friendly passer by yelled out "Hey lady you've got a flat tire!" Alysia retorted" I have three full ones that will get me to the gas station!" Life has its starts and stops and instead of letting the days events get her down she just kept on going, focusing on solutions and never letting anything dampen her day.

6) Believe in yourself, in others, and in the impossible. Believing in yourself means that you hold yourself in high esteem. It means that you validate your accomplishments and celebrate your successes. It also means that you honor yourself. You take time for your needs and wants, and you care for and about yourself. In addition, it means that you are willing to go for the "seemingly impossible," that which appears unreasonable to even imagine wanting.

After a lovely dinner Robert and three friends took a cab home only to discover that he had left his bag in the taxi. Michael one of the passengers, realizing the situation, sprinted down the street after the cab. Realizing the taxi was out of sight, he turned around and followed his message to turn down the first side street. There off to the side was the cab with the bag on the seat where Robert had been seated. Michael opened the door, reclaimed the bag and gave the driver a reward for handing it over. That evening Michael made the seemingly impossible happen!

7)   Be committed to moving in your life; reach out for help and/or have a coaching session when you get off track or "stuck."

8)   Love yourself unconditionally; all the parts of you; and treasure who you are. Conditional love means that you accept yourself only when you live up to the expectations and standards that you and others have established. When your body looks the way it should, when you produce the results that you have stipulated, when you have manifested the ideal relationship, and when your life is the perfect picture of success, then and only then can you accept yourself. When you love yourself unconditionally, you love and accept yourself when areas of your life are imperfect. When you are sick in bed you still love yourself. When a big deal has fallen through, you still love and accept yourself. When you have a fight with your best friend, you still love and accept yourself. When you let someone down, break an agreement, or unknowingly hurt someone, you still love and accept yourself. It is about treasuring who you are and honoring your relationship with yourself. When you don't live up to your standards, you look and see what the lessons are, learn them, and let go.

Nicolette's son was at risk in school and was in danger of having to repeat his first year of high school. In her session with me she realized her reaction to his failing grades was getting in his way. In addition, she was blaming herself for being a bad parent. Once she realized this, she chose to focus on being a stabilizing force with limited reactions. She had raised and supported him in following his dreams. She could love herself unconditionally even if his grades never reached the optimum levels.

9)   Pursue your dreams, your inspiration, your "higher self," and your messages. Going for your dreams may not always be convenient. Life presents us with tests and lessons that beg the question, "How much do you want this?" When you go after your dreams, inspiration and messages you realize that you will be asked to stretch into larger shoes

than you ever imagined. If you are going to be an example to others, you need to lead others to their inspiration. When you can't seem to write the story, find the time to get the project done, or breakthrough your own explanations, you use your own coach to support you through the challenges and make it happen.

Brandon sat down in front of me. He confided, " I've wanted be a wine maker all my life." What's in the way," I probed. "Three small children, a life in another country, and a high powered banker wife who would need to agree. I love the feel and the smell of the vines, being in nature and I am passionate about Normandy. I was there last summer and it was an incredible experience. I would love to return." As we sat together he shared that he was going to be on holiday in Normandy for a week and could take the first steps of the research process to see if there was a job opportunity in his dream region. He found his desire, a long-range plan and his courage; then he recruited his wife and the whole family to go with him to explore the opportunities in France.

10) Reach out to others and a higher power when you need support. Ask for help, guidance and direction.

11) To be responsible for your actions and take charge of situations which you are able to resolve positively.

12) Regard everything in your life as a mirror, to learn lessons, to grow, to search for the perfection in the grand scheme of things and to lovingly self-correct.

Your commitment to growth must be more important than your need to be perfect. Neither pride, nor stubbornness blocks you from seeing, discovering, and growing every facet of your life. Seeing the perfection is not always easy. To see the perfection, you must have some perspective and an elevated viewpoint. When you see the perfection, you examine the situation from the point of view of being essential to teach you a lesson that otherwise you might not learn.

excerpted from *Transformational Life Coaching* by Dr. Chérie Carter-Scott, MCC and Lynn U. Stewart, PCC, hcibooks.com 2007

David Steele, MA, MFT, CPC

David Steele, MA, MFT, CPC is a Marriage and Family Therapist who fell in love with coaching and in 1997 founded Relationship Coaching Institute, the first and largest international relationship coach training organization. He's the author of The Million Dollar Private Practice (Wiley, 2011) and From Therapist to Coach (Wiley, 2011), both are available on Amazon.com. One of David's mottos is The More People You Help, the More Money You Make, and he's an unabashed advocate of helping coaches leverage their expertise to earn six and seven figures while making a significant difference in the world as a popular speaker, coach and consultant on innovative marketing and business building systems and strategies.

David's websites include:
www.relationshipcoachinginstitute.com
www.milliondollarpractice.net
www.therapist2coach.com

CHAPTER 3

THE #1 SECRET OF BUILDING A MILLION DOLLAR COACHING PRACTICE

David Steele, MA, MFT, CPC

Let's start this ambitious chapter with some brutal honesty gleaned from my 20 years in the coaching profession:

Anyone can call himself or herself a "coach"
Many who call themselves "coach" have no professional coach training
Many coaches enter this profession with the greatest of intentions, but are coming from ego rather than service (more about this below)
The public, for the most part, is aware of the above and leery of coaching
And lastly, most new coaches struggle and eventually wash out

These are disturbing truths, but if we are to be successful we must first be crystal clear about our challenges and what doesn't work.

Given the above, why are you reading this book? What motivates you to become a coach despite the challenges and obstacles?

For most of us, it's simple; we're driven to help others and make a difference in the world.

Ego vs. Service
The desire to help others is among the most noble, however this desire tends to be driven by either ego or service.
Ego motivates people to help others as a way to gain status, power, money, control, validation, and self-esteem.

Service motivates people to help others from a selfless calling to a higher mission.

And then there's the biggest paradox of coaching- the public and untrained coaches often believe coaching is about giving people advice, while trained coaches understand that giving advice is futile and arrogant.

But who doesn't enjoy giving people advice? What's wrong with advice? Those who believe they know the answers and others should follow their advice are coming from ego. Untrained coaches can be a bit like the delusional bad singer on American Idol who truly believes that they have an excellent voice and that they're exceptionally talented and should be awarded fame and fortune for sharing their "gift" with the rest of us. Untrained coaches don't understand that reading books, listening to CDs, attending workshops, life experience, and even having a college degree does not qualify them or give them the skills to competently help others with their most important life goals and challenges.

Feeling a bit offended or uncomfortable reading this? Do you believe you should be richly rewarded for your advice? Then stop reading this chapter right now as there's no need to waste your time.

Are you willing to let go of ego and advice-giving to truly be of service? Wonderful. Let's explore how to be a highly successful coach.

Who Do You Serve?

The most important factor in your success is being crystal clear about who you serve, also referred to as your "niche" or "tribe." This is your target audience for your marketing and services.

Your niche is different from your profession or specialty. Your profession might be "Relationship Coach" and your specialty might be "Dating After Divorce." This is "what" you do.

Your niche is "who" you serve and the biggest challenge for many new coaches is narrowing the possibilities from "everyone in the world" to an identifiable group of people you can reach and serve, such as "newly divorced singles in Atlanta, GA."

Once you've identified your niche clearly and narrowly, then you can design your marketing and services for them using The Platinum Rule, which is my #1 secret of success in business and in life.

The Golden Rule vs. The Platinum Rule of Business and Marketing

The Golden Rule states "Do unto others as you would have them do unto you." Conversely, "Don't do to others what you wouldn't want for yourself." While this practice civilizes us and helps us get along in society, it doesn't work in marketing and building a service-oriented business.

Here's an analogy; if you wanted to give someone a present and you followed this rule, you would give them something you would like to receive, which only works if they're exactly like you! However well-meaning and unintentional, the message you're sending your target audience is:

"I care more about what's important to me than what's important to you."

Ouch! Most coaches don't intend to send this message at all!

The Platinum Rule states "Do unto others as they want to be done to." To do so requires connecting with others and learning what they really want, rather than what you want to provide them.

This works great for sex; you're much more likely to pleasure your partner by doing what feels good for them rather than what feels good for you. Your sales will be much higher by providing programs and services that address what your customers want rather than what you think they need. Your message to your target audience is:

"I genuinely care about what's important to you."

This is the #1 Secret of Powerful, Irresistible, and Effective Marketing That Gets Results

Many coaches understand this yet seem to have a hard time implementing it. I've seen many excitedly launch their coaching business and their marketing flops. It pains me to see such passionate, talented, well intentioned professionals struggle to make a living because they have such a hard time connecting with the people they want to serve.

Market Research: The Key to Guaranteed Success

I cannot overstate the value of conducting market research. In fact, along with a few other key factors, credible market research is what differentiates successful coaches from unsuccessful coaches.

Market research starts with learning core relevant facts about your niche. Who are they? Where are they? What do they want? What works for them? What doesn't work for them? How are they being served (if at all) by other services? Ultimately, you want your market research to help you create a profile of your ideal client. And by ideal I don't mean the nicest or the one who will send you the most referrals. Sure, that's ideal, but not in the sense that it's being used here. Rather, you want to clearly picture who it is that you're serving. You want to understand what motivates them and what doesn't, what they're striving for, what they consider success to be (because it may not be the same as what you think it is, or even, what you think it should be), and so on.

Quality market research is done through 1:1 conversations with people that fit your niche, or through a focus group. And let me say bluntly: surveys are useless! Especially email or online surveys sent to a large group. The information you receive won't help you. You need qualitative information, not quantitative numbers. Your goal is to learn about your niche from the inside out and get to know them so well that it becomes clear how to market to them and what services to provide. Email and online surveys won't do this. Got it?!

Ideally, you'll conduct market research continuously on your existing programs, new programs, ideas for programs, and so on. Just as large corporations use market research to effectively market and serve their customers, this is a key to your success.

Five Steps for Coaches Conducting Market Research

Step One: Research your niche for their demographic information, other professionals/organizations that serve them, other approaches to helping them, websites, online social networking groups, books, workshops, and so on. Call or meet with similar and complementary professionals and organizations to learn more about how they help the people in your niche. Do your homework and become an expert on available information about your target clients.

Step Two: Put together some ideas for programs, branding, services, and so on. Create a variety of program names to find out which they prefer. A great exercise is to brainstorm answers to this question: "If I were to write a book or deliver a workshop for my niche, what would I call it?"

Step Three: Identify 3-5 people who fit your niche. Ideally, these are people you know. If not, then ask your network for referrals. Contact them for informational interviews.

Step Four: Conduct your informational interviews and ask for feedback about your ideas from Step Two. Ask what they read, where they hang out, what groups and organizations they join, what publications they subscribe to, and so on. Ask them about their experiences, needs, goals, and challenges. Ask them about what they've done, where they've gone, who they've worked with to get support for the need or goal you will address in your business. Listen very closely to the language they use to describe their needs and goals. Ask for their top three problems and top three goals. Ask them to describe their ideal support service or program to address their need or goal.

Step Five: Compile your data and ideas, and use them to design the services, branding, and programs for your niche. Follow up with your market research participants and get their feedback on your ideas, plus ask them for referrals. Remember: an important principle is that "people support what they help create," and when you follow-up with those who helped you along the way, you'll be pleasantly surprised by their excitement and support. In fact, a common and delightful by-product is that some of them might sign up for your program!

Reminder - DO NOT USE SURVEYS! Re-read the above for an

explanation if needed.

Reminder - DO NOT IGNORE YOUR MARKET RESEARCH and do what sounds good to you (this is all too common)

While the above might sound like a lot of work, it's time well spent that will be critical to your success. Short cuts just don't work.

From Frustrated Therapist to Successful Coach (My Story)

In 1996 I was burning out in my private practice as a Marriage and Family Therapist working with couples on the verge of divorce when I stumbled upon this emerging new profession of personal or life coaching. Suspicious, but intrigued, I signed up for a weekend training with one of the most prominent coach training programs I could find and was blown away. I continued my training and obtained certification.

Convinced that coaching is the next evolution for promoting successful relationships, I was shocked that I couldn't find a relationship coach training program, not one. So with new eyes and an open mind I set about adapting what I learned about coaching to relationships, and immediately experienced an epiphany- "Singles become couples."

Of course! As a therapist it never occurred to me to do anything with singles, but as a coach it was completely logical to target a huge audience that strongly desires what I want to help them achieve; a lifelong, fulfilling relationship.

But I knew nothing about helping singles. Reading self-help books by self-styled experts and gurus for singles about how to flirt, how to dress, what to say to "get" the guy or girl just made me sick to my stomach.

So how to proceed? How can I be of service to this target audience I know nothing about? Out of desperation I gathered a group of singles willing to come to my office for a 4-week focus group, which ended up being the smartest thing I've ever done for my business as a private practice professional.

That focus group helped me "get" what singles in my area really want and need, so when I launched my new relationship coaching business over the next few weeks, it was wildly successful and I had a full coaching practice within 90 days (which might sound like hype, but it's absolutely true, I even have witnesses!).

I finally was experiencing the highly successful practice I've always wanted, which caught the attention of my local MFT colleagues who requested that I train them. My initial response was "NO!" as I was having a lot of fun with my practice and never desired to train anyone in anything. Then, feeling a higher calling and responsibility to contribute to making the world a better place (which is why I became a therapist/coach) I put together an introductory weekend workshop and Relationship Coaching Institute, was born, which became the first and largest international relationship coach training organization.

Eventually I put together what I learned about coaching singles into my book "Conscious Dating," followed by a book for coaching couples "Radical Marriage." I was approached by the publisher John Wiley & Sons to write a book for therapists about coaching that became "From Therapist to Coach," followed by compiling what I learned about building a highly successful coaching practice into "The Million Dollar Private Practice," also published by Wiley.

All this happened because, like you, I wanted to help people and make a difference in the world, and was called to this profession (coaching) and a specialty (singles) that I knew nothing about, and approached my new business with a completely open mind and sincere desire to be of service. I followed the above 5 steps for conducting market research, and you can too!

A Word of Warning

I've seen many smart coaches acknowledge the wisdom of conducting marketing research to build their business and then ignore their data and fail or struggle as a result. Why? My guess is that it's efficient, convenient and psychologically satisfying -- a deadly trio when it points the wrong way - to build your business around what "sounds good" or "seems right" to you. Our ego is insidious and the Golden Rule is ingrained in us.

Regardless of how good your hunches are or how many times you're right about things, my advice to you is to always conduct your market research first, and then design your services, programs, and marketing on the hard data that you generate. If this merely verifies what you already "guessed," then more power to you. But more often than not, your market research will re-shape your hypotheses; if not outright obliterate them (a humbling, yet staggeringly informative experience).

The other way of remembering all of the above - the more fun, positive way - is simply this: market to your target audience, not to yourself. And make no mistake: you are not your target market. This is one of the biggest flaws in all marketing (by no means limited to coaches). Often, businesses of all sizes forget that they aren't their target market. Or to put it differently: they assume that they are their target market. So they simply say to themselves: "Hey, this makes sense to me, so it must make sense to the people I'm trying to communicate with."

Of course all of the above depends upon understanding the need to identify your niche as your target audience for your services. You can't effectively market to and help anyone and everyone; you must target your marketing to your specific, desired audience.

So practice the Platinum Rule in your business, conduct your market research, and design your services, programs, and marketing for your desired audience, and you're almost guaranteed to be a wildly successful coach!

Donna Stoneham, Ph.D.

Donna Stoneham, Ph.D. Certified Integral Coach® is a master executive coach, author, transformational leadership expert, speaker, and popular media guest who lives in Northern California. For over twenty-five years, she's guided several thousand Fortune 500 and not-for profit leaders, teams, and organizations to unleash their power to thrive™ in work and life. Donna is the author of the award winning book, The Thriver's Edge: Seven Keys to Transform the Way You Live, Love, and Lead named by BuzzFeed as "Nine Awesome Books for your Kick-Ass Career." Donna has been featured in the Wall Street Journal, TD Magazine and Investor's Business Daily. She is President of Positive Impact, LLC www.positiveimpactllc.com and co-creator of Integral Intelligence® www.integraliq.com and is featured as one of the world's leading coaches in the documentary, Leap, The Coaching Movie (2017). Take Donna's Thriver Quiz at www.DonnaStoneham.com and follow her at donnastoneham@twitter.com and DonnaStonehamPhD@facebook.com.

CHAPTER 4

BRING YOUR WHOLE SELF TO WORK: USING INTEGRAL INTELLIGENCE® TO THRIVE AS A COACH AND CREATE A SUSTAINABLE COACHING PRACTICE

Donna Stoneham, Ph.D.

The process of becoming a leader is much the same as the process of becoming a fully integrated human being. – Warren Bennis1

I am blessed to have the greatest job on earth–coaching leaders to create transformational results that enable them to unleash their power to thrive in work and life and help others to do the same. Since 1993, I've been fortunate to guide several thousand leaders, executives, and teams in their development efforts in my role as an executive coach, transformational leadership consultant, and educator. Before that, I spent ten years in various leadership roles in corporate America.

The sad fact is that 68% of workers in America and 87% worldwide are not engaged at work.2 I am a firm believer in the "ripple effect," and how, as we transform ourselves, we inspire others to do the same. When people feel valued, aligned, and engaged with their work, amazing things happen. My purpose as a coach is to support those I serve to use their talents and realize their aspirations in ways that create a ripple effect in their families, teams, and in the organizations they serve so they can make a positive impact in the world.

Being a coach has helped me to realize my own aspirations of helping others unleash their potential in ways that help create a world where all can thrive. Every day is a new challenge, a new opportunity, and a new adventure as I watch the leaders I'm blessed to work with grow into the people and leaders they seek to become.

The Warren Bennis quote above speaks to what's required to become an exceptional leader. The same can be said of what's required to become an excellent coach, regardless of the coaching arena in which you choose to work. Becoming a great coach and developing a sustainable coaching practice also requires becoming a fully integrated being. We must do the work we are asking others to do, and be willing to be authentic and vulnerable ourselves. This stance to coaching enables the creation of a powerful, two-way relationship that's grounded on mutual trust and respect.

There are several things that help us do that. First, we have to be willing to do our own work, bring all of our wisdom to bear, and model what we teach. Second, we have to find our niche and work from our sweet spot, rather than trying to be all things to all people. Third, we have to learn to listen to the insights we offer our clients and apply them to ourselves. And finally, we need to try and pay it forward by seeking to leave a legacy that is bigger than ourselves.

Be Your Best Self: Seek to Model What You Teach
The most important thing I've learned in my experience coaching leaders and executives is that we are most powerful coaching others when we're able to access and use all aspects of our intelligence, stay connected to our purpose, and lead and coach authentically.

In our Integral Intelligence® work, we teach leaders in organizations how to effectively coach others. In order to be an excellent coach, you have to model what you teach, or you won't have credibility. By the nature of our work, as coaches, we are leaders, because the people we serve look to us as guides of behavior they seek to embody themselves. So there needs to be alignment between our words, behaviors, and beliefs in order for that to happen.

How we show up with our clients matters. The cognitive aspects necessary for coaching are important (technical skills, using grounded theory and inquiry in our work), but the capacity to be fully present with our clients separates average from exceptional coaches, whether we are leaders coaching other people or coaches coaching leaders. That requires developing the capacity to tap into our emotional, relational, somatic, and spiritual intelligence.

Cognitive and emotional intelligence are only part of the equation for success as a coach or a leader. In 2002, with 50 years of corporate leadership experience between us, my colleague Pat Weger and I sought to crack the code to leadership development that created powerful business results, while deepening leadership effectiveness and engagement. We designed a model we call Integral Intelligence® which we've been using with executive coaching clients and leadership teams for fourteen years.3 Our model includes helping clients develop, integrate, and unleash all five aspects of leadership intelligence: 1) cognitive-the wisdom of the mind 2) emotional-the wisdom of the heart 3) relational-the wisdom of engagement 4) somatic-the wisdom of the body and 5) spiritual-the wisdom of connection.

We created this context because it's not only the functional skills of what you do as a leader or coach that counts, it's also who you are. We call this "way-of-being."

In our experience, what differentiated good, or not-so-good, leaders and coaches from great ones was how they showed up, especially in the midst of challenge, change, and complexity. We designed a process that supports leaders as coaches to close this gap between their "way-of-doing" and "way-of-being" by guiding them to reflect on their patterns of behavior, challenge their world-view, deepen self-insight, and focus on how they show up in every moment, interaction, and response. We help them build the capacity to be mindful in their work as leaders and coaches every day.

35 | Donna Stoneham, Ph.D.

The Integral Intelligence® Model

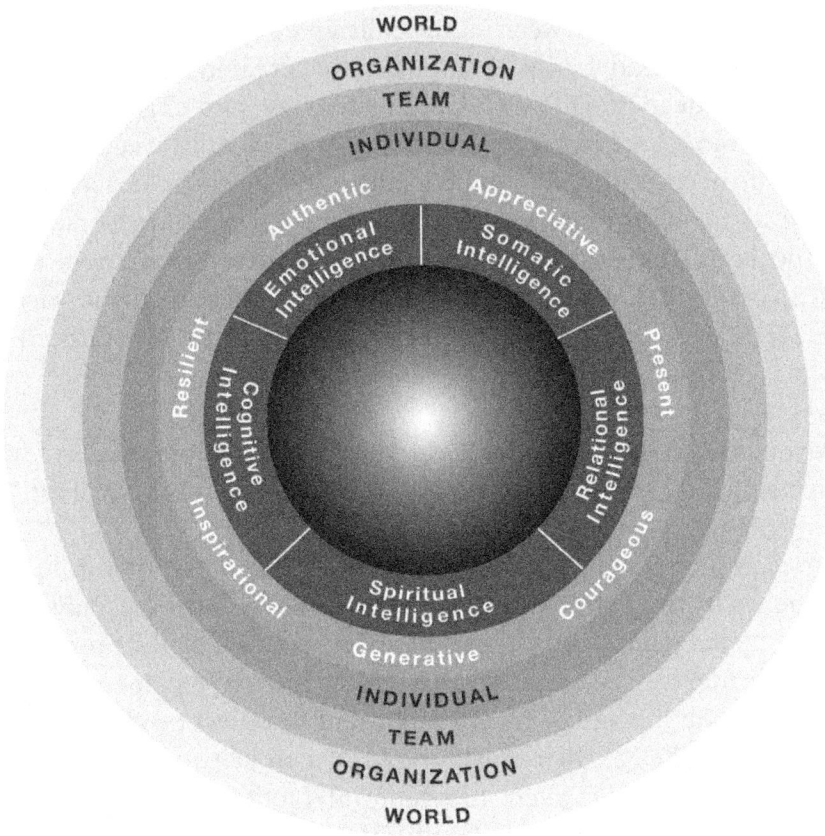

As coaches and leaders, when we develop and deepen our ability to use multiple sources of intelligence in our work and lives, it helps us build our capacity to be more:

Resilient: Able to maintain high energy levels, to stay centered in the midst of conflict and bounce back quickly from stressful situations or defeat.

Generative: Able to ask powerful questions and to catalyze insight, creativity and action in others.

Present: Able to listen and engage in conversations and interactions with others so they feel valued and respected.

Authentic: Able to model genuineness and transparency in a way that fosters trust and invites openness from others.

Courageous: Able to take risks that lead to expansion and growth while being accountable for the results of one's actions.

Appreciative: Able to see possibilities, build from strengths, and accelerate positive energy.

Inspirational: The ability to stimulate, motivate and encourage others to aspire to achieve personal and/or collective goals.

Leaders as coaches learn a new frame of reference for more effective action as they stop falling into old, unconscious traps of default behaviors and step up to lead and coach with integral intelligence. Here are some of the ways they make those shifts:

Stepping Up to Lead with Integral Intelligence®

Traps Leaders Fall Into	How to Step Out
Relying on cognitive intelligence	Use all dimensions of intelligence
Habitual patterns drive actions	Self insight informs behavior
Fragmented work and life	Integrate experience
Orienting around problems	Create possibilities
Motivated by personal gain	Unleash potential in others
Focusing on short term success	Foster sustainable outcomes
Driven by deliverables	Inspire meaning in work
Burning out	Maintain resilience
Playing a role defined by others	Be authentic
Scattered attention	Present in the moment
Delivering the answers	Ask powerful questions
Performing as expert	Facilitate learning
Spinning the message	Tell the truth
Operating in siloes	Focus on the greater good
Limited by circumstances	Catalyze change

©Integral Intelligence

As we learn to utilize all five aspects of our intelligence, we deepen our self-sight and can model what we teach. We learn to skillfully inquire to challenge others and our own assumptions. As we're willing to be vulnerable with the people we coach, we give them the permission to follow our lead. The capacity and desire to keep learning, growing, and challenging ourselves to be the best that we can be as coaches inspires those we serve to want to do the same.

Reflection Questions:

1. As you reflect on these five aspects of intelligence (cognitive, emotional, relational, spiritual and somatic) how would you rate yourself in terms of your own development on a scale of 1 (low)–5 (high)? What are some actions you could take to develop the aspects of intelligence you'd like to enhance? How might you leverage those aspects of intelligence in which you're strongest in your coaching?
2. Of these qualities (being resilient, generative, present, authentic, courageous, appreciative and inspirational) which do you consistently demonstrate as a coach? Which do you need to continue to develop? What are some steps you could take?

Claim it and Name It: Work from Your Sweet Spot

I left the corporate world in the early 90's after a ten-year career as a leader in managed health care to start my own organizational development consulting and coaching practice. At the time, I was a Regional Vice President of a mail-order pharmacy company in sales and marketing. I'd been through two mergers and acquisitions, resulting in three jobs and two lay-offs in one year. It was as if the universe was telling me, "It's time to get off this bus!"

So I did what many people do. I made business cards, culled through my contacts, and let people know I was venturing out on my own. In the first few years, I accepted just about any job that came across the transom. Coaching as a profession was not yet popular, so for several years, I lived paycheck to paycheck. I learned a lot about entrepreneurship, but I wasn't really thriving. In my corporate career, I'd worked in several dysfunctional organizations and wanted to be part of the solution. A few years later, I bought an assessment tool franchise. That enabled me to work with teams and leaders using the tools to coach them in organizations, but I still felt restricted.

My strongest intelligences are spiritual, relational, and emotional. In the early days of my coaching practice, I was afraid if I brought my authentic self to my engagements I'd be rejected, because I didn't believe the corporate world would value what I offered. So I kept taking jobs and working with leaders with whose values and missions I wasn't aligned. In the late 90's, I began working on my graduate degree in transformative learning. I loved my academic work because of its depth, but it made me feel even more disconnected from what I was doing. I was yearning to do work with more meaning.

In the early 2000's, I attended a workshop where I discovered Appreciate Inquiry, a participatory method of resolving issues, envisioning brighter futures, and creating positive change in teams and organizations. I felt like I'd come home and found a way to facilitate the kind of change that I'd been seeking. At the workshop, we were asked to introduce ourselves with a graphic that included a symbol of the role we played in our work. That day was a turning point in my career because I drew a symbol of Joan of Arc on a horse with a line drawn across her as in a "no smoking" sign. I introduced myself that day as someone who, for the past ten years, had been trying to root out the perpetrators and rescue the victims in my work. I realized in that moment, that no matter what the cost, that was no longer the role I wanted to play. That wasn't the "brand" I wanted to stand for.

Planting my flag in the sand that day started a cascade of deep change. Within six months, I lost all my corporate clients. I had the worst year in revenues I'd ever experienced. I had to refinance our house to live, but by the end of that year, I had replaced every client I had lost and I was doing work that brought me joy with people who shared my values and appreciated my work. After an intense, transformational, year-long coaches training program at New Ventures West in San Francisco, I was certified as an Integral Coach® and teamed up with a friend and colleague I met in my coaching program. We collaborated and created the model and the content for our Integral Intelligence® work. We soon landed our first corporate client and I was able to start doing the deep, transformational work I'd been longing to do with a Fortune 100 group of high-potential leaders.

When I made the decision to stop trying to be all things to all people and truly honor my gifts, my life and practice opened up in ways I'd never expected. I began to experience financial abundance and deep joy. I began to live for my work, rather than working just to live.

Now I am clear about my value-add. I tell prospective clients that I work holistically, that the work is transformational and strengths-based. I explain my methodology up-front, share why I love my work and what my sweet spot is, and no longer hold anything back. I commit to my clients that I will be present to them wherever they are and that every aspect of their lives is fodder for coaching. My style and approach helps leaders discern and self-select if what I offer is the right fit for them.

Over the years, I've mentored new coaches, entrepreneurs, MBA students and leaders. The advice I always give them is to find their sweet spot and work from that place. If you're good at leadership development, then name it and claim it as the focus of your coaching practice. If you are a powerful strategist, then be a strategic coach. If your gift is knowing how to start new businesses, be a better parent, have better relationships, or create a more meaningful life, then claim your niche and do that. But be true to who you are, to what you value most deeply, and to doing the kind of coaching work that allows you to express your greatest gifts and experience joy. Don't try and be all things to all people. Find your sweet spot and nothing can hold you back from achieving your goals and building a thriving coaching practice.

ReflectionQuestions:

1. What is your sweet spot in coaching?
2. In your business?
3. How do you know that is true?

A Practice for Coaches:

If you aren't sure about your sweet spot, ask those you coach why they chose to work with you. What is it about your style or methodology that intrigued them? Likewise, when you complete a coaching engagement, ask your clients what they found most valuable about the work you did together. This accomplishes two things. First, it gives you greater insight into the kinds of people and organizations who might resonate with your work. Second, it literally helps you understand and be able to better articulate your "brand."

Heed Your Own Advice: Practice What You Preach

The relationship between coaches and coaching clients presents a transformational opportunity for both parties. I think of the coach-coaching client relationship like a potter working with clay. Sometimes as a coach, you are the potter, and sometimes, you are the vessel being formed. The same holds true for the coaching client. As coaches and coaching clients, we make impressions on one another that help us both grow and evolve. When that happens, the coaching relationship becomes a "win-win" for both parties. There is a balance of power, insights are revealed, and change occurs through the wisdom that both parties glean through the relationship. The coaching relationship helps both parties enhance our emotional, spiritual, relational, cognitive and somatic intelligence.

In my coaching journal I keep what I call my "talk to the hand" page. I use it to document insights I have for my clients that I would benefit from applying in my own work and life. For example, if I'm talking to a client about how to better integrate work and life by taking better care of themselves on a day when I've gotten five hours of sleep after working for seven days straight, I will enter the advice I gave my client in my "talk to the hand" page as coaching advice for myself. Likewise, if I offer a coaching practice to a client to do that would also benefit me, I write that down in my journal as a way to keep me in check.

One of the biggest issues my executive coaching clients face is reclaiming balance in their lives. Often the first thing that disappears in the lives of busy leaders is taking care of themselves in ways that enable them to be their best at work and with their families. The second thing that often gets sacrificed are their support networks. Offering "anchor practices" that help them better integrate work and life and making sure they have an adequate support network at their disposal are critically important to deepen their effectiveness and engagement. Some of the "anchor practices" I offer my clients are things like taking a walk at lunch; engaging in centering practices such as mindfulness meditation, tai chi or yoga; exercising regularly, and spending quality time each week with family and friends. I try and give them practices that help deepen multiple sources of intelligence, like taking a yoga class (emotional, somatic, spiritual and relational).

In order to inspire our coaching clients to make the changes they seek to make in their lives, as coaches, we need to model the behaviors we espouse. One of the things I've learned from running a successful coaching practice is that too much of a good thing can be a bad thing. Because most people who embark on coaching as a profession do so because of a genuine desire to help others, we have to be mindful of the boundaries of time and energy we need to claim for ourselves. We need to create and nurture regular self-care rituals and support systems that allow us to be our best. Great coaches don't do this work alone. Joining professional coaching associations, starting a mastermind group, or joining a case study group with other coaches can be help you hone your coaching skills as well as serve as part of your support network.

As a coach, I do not view myself as the all-knowing expert. I trust my clients know what is best for themselves. My job is to be a way-shower and guide to help them discover what they may already know, but may have forgotten on their climb up the corporate ladder. I may be fifteen minutes ahead of them on some things, but they are fifteen minutes ahead of me on others. My job is to ask generative questions that help them stretch and grow and that may illuminate a blind spot they may have. Likewise, I listen to the questions I ask to see if I need to ask them of myself.

Reflection Questions:

1. As you reflect on the coaching conversations you've had with clients over the past month, what are some of the practices, resources, reflection questions or advice that you've offered your clients which you would benefit from applying yourself? In what ways might you begin to do that? How will you know you've been successful?

2. Every day, ask yourself, "Is my life mirroring the message I seek to convey to the clients I serve?" If it not, then what do you need to change and how?

A Practice for Coaches:

Keep a small journal or notebook in your purse or pocket. When you have an insight working with a coaching client that you would benefit from applying yourself, write it down. After your coaching session, design a practice or reflection questions for yourself, just as you would for a coaching client. Engaging in this practice will help you accomplish the following. First, it will help you offer greater support to the person you're coaching because you'll have personal experience working on this issue. Second, it will help you grow and evolve as a coach and human being. Third, it will give you a way to keep track of coaching practices and reflection questions which may be helpful for future coaching clients.

Leave a Legacy: Pay It Forward:

One of the questions we ask the leaders we work with in our leadership development programs is, "Who is the leader you're seeking to become?" The same question can be asked of coaches. "Who is the coach you're seeking to become?" What kind of mark do you want to make on the world with your work? What is the ripple effect you want to create in the work and lives of those you serve?

As coaches, the impact we make in the lives of those we coach creates a chain reaction. I often tell my clients when they get better at work, they get better at home and vice versa. So when you help a mother be a better leader, you also support her to be a better mother. When you teach another person, through your example, how to be a better leader, coach, or mentor, you never know how many lives that person's life will touch.

What I've learned over the years in my practice is to worry less about how much money I make and focus my energies on the kind of difference I want to make in the lives of those I serve. If you focus on doing your best work, being true to yourself, and bringing your whole self to work, the money will follow. The transformation in your clients' lives and the stories they tell will sell you and be your leverage point for success.

Reflection Questions:

1) What is the legacy that you want to create with your coaching business? In your work as a coach?
2) What is the difference that you want to make in the world and how can you pay it forward?
3) In what ways can you bring all of your intelligence to bear in making the world a better place, regardless of the venues in which you work or the type of coaching you do?

Carol Koziol, MA, PCC

As an ICF Professional Certified Coach, *Carol Koziol* guides people who have started to become a little less young to find the courage to uncover and live into their own "What's Next." Nature is an integral part of Carol's Natural Courage™ approach. Reconnecting to ourselves through nature enables you to shed the issues disguising your true path forward. With the process of clarity, creativity, and choice you learn to create heart-centered changes while exercising your Natural Courage muscles moving you towards your "What's Next".

As an Entrepreneur, Mother, Earth Explorer and PhD Candidate, Carol understands the challenges of navigating change and transition. Her background includes working with thousands of people in over three hundred businesses spanning careers in Health and Fitness, IT Technical Training, Business Consulting, Project Management, Workshop Facilitation and Professional Coaching.

Natural Courage, Inc.
ICF Professional Coaching
Integrative Enneagram Assessments
Facilitation & Natureshops
www.naturalcourage.com

CHAPTER 5

NATURAL COURAGE: CREATING A BUSINESS WITH CLARITY, CREATIVITY, AND CHOICE

Carol Koziol, MA, PCC

We all have problem somethings in our life or business that could use some *natural courage* to resolve. Whatever the situation, I have found that the three common components of *clarity, creativity,* and *choice* have applied to my coaching approach as well as my business development. When a challenge is viewed with complete clarity, creative options or solutions become more obvious, and then informed choices are easier to make.

The following are a few stories about how I became a Professional Coach, how Natural Courage became a business, and *three* actions you can implement to create more growth on your business journey. Also, since coaching is all about personal development and collaborative relationships, I will not pretend to have done everything alone and will fully share some of those who helped catalyze the major changes in my life and business.

From Business Consulting to Life Coaching

When my youngest son left for University my life radically changed. As an empty nester I embraced the opportunity to complete a full life review and of course this included my career. With the support of my very first coach, Marcia Hyatt, we easily identified the deep gladness which I derived from working with people. This theme had percolated throughout my career as a YMCA staff member, a corporate technology trainer, a software solutions specialist, and a small business consultant.

Carol Koziol, MA, PCC

With a Master's degree in Physical Education, a Certificate in Management, and 25 years' experience working with over 300 companies, I had learned how to actively listen and intuitively nudge people towards change. However, as with my other career shifts, I had strategically decided that to become a *professional* coach it would be wise to acquire some *professional* training. And so I completed an International Coach Federation (ICF) accredited training program with Adler International Learning in Toronto, Canada.

Yes there were a lot of similarities between coaching and the business / management / organizational development world that I had been exposed to over the years ... *but* there were also many significant differences. It took many hours of practice to ensure that I could smoothly demonstrate all eleven ICF core competencies within every coaching session. I still clearly remember one of my first coaching mentors, Sue Sheldon, suggesting that I laminate those ICF core competencies so I could stick them under my pillow and 'sleep on them'. Even today I am not afraid to share that I regularly review my notes in order to keep my coaching technique sharp and focused.

The other big learning for me was becoming aware of the major differences between Coaching, Consulting, Counselling, Training, and Mentoring. For many years I was a successful Consultant ... you know the expert with the slides and all the answers. Of course professional coaching is about partnering with clients in a creative process inspiring them to maximize their personal and professional potential, in other words guiding clients to find their *own* solutions.

This was a huge shift for me (and my ego). I had to accept that I did not know all the answers. Now when working with clients, the role I represent is always clearly identified. If a client requests both coaching and consulting I make it abundantly clear which hat is being worn before I speak. Sometimes I even carry a pink ball cap which I take on and off to signify coaching versus consulting. This makes sessions less confusing for the client.

Over the past eight years I have honed my skills as a Coach becoming an ICF Professional Certified Coach (PCC). Similar to other licensed practitioners such as therapists and counsellors, there is a code of ethics which all ICF members must abide by. The maintenance of this designation requires Continuing Coach Education (CCE) units. Belonging to the ICF holds my feet to the fire so to speak, forcing me to keep my coaching skillset current and relevant.

Furthermore, because of the requirement for continual professional development, I have expanded my learning to include; certification as a Positrak Team Coaching Specialist, a Certified Integrativ Enneagram Practitioner, a Certified Ecotherapist, a Work-That-Reconnects Facilitator, and I have just recently completed a Master's degree in Depth Psychology. *How are you professionally developing and keeping your skillset sharp?*

From Blogging to Business

While I was studying to become a professional coach I began to blog about my other passion, the natural world. Writing about our inner and outer landscapes generated a lot of interest and created a bunch of followers. This was when the entity Natural Courage was born.

Courage generally means a quality of mind or spirit that enables a person to face danger, difficulty, uncertainty, or pain without becoming overcome by fear or deflected from a chosen course of action. A little more research uncovered that at its root the word "cor" was the Latin word for heart. Also, I found an obsolete definition of courage to represent the heart being the source of emotion. So when you do let your heart speak, you are being naturally courageous by moving more confidently forward in new directions. This totally described me and my coaching approach ... reconnecting people to their natural world, internally and externally through heart-centered change.

During the first few years I would eagerly coach anyone within a three foot radius that would listen to me. This was fabulous for my coaching confidence but definitely not a great business strategy. Since I truly wanted to do more coaching and less consulting, it was time for me to get a little more serious about my business approach. Engaging the services of Chris Williams, a small business coach from Wide Awake Business, we worked together through one their customer generator programs ... and this made all the difference.

In the next section I will share three business activities behind Clarity, Creativity, and Choice which just might help your coaching / business practice. These activities include; uncovering your superpower, speaking your clients' language, and working a daily power hour.

Clarity: *What is Your Superpower?*

One of the things I loved about working with my business coach Chris, was that she put things into clear and simple terms avoiding heavy marketing lingo. When she asked me to describe what my *superpower* was – at first I had no clue. But eventually the answer was obvious, my superpower was *Natural Courage*.

Coaching people to create heart-centered change through reconnection to their natural world aptly described my superpower. My unique process included *clarity, creativity,* and *choice*. I also used nature as a modality and as a metaphor in all aspects of my coaching and personal development practice. Through *natural courage* I leveraged lessons from the natural world to catalyze heart-centered change. Whether the session was a walk-and-talk or an online natural nudge, the intersection of people and nature was my superpower. It is where I do my best work and has always been where I am the happiest, personally and professionally.

Some people would refer to this as their niche, others would mention mission statement, and some would even liken it to their sweet spot. Regardless of what you resonate with, the fact of the matter is that according to a 2016 ICF Global Coaching Study, there are over 53,300 coaches in the world and with coaching becoming one of the fastest growing professions there is a lot of competition. Many of us have at least one or two post-secondary degrees, years of business experience, some of us have coaching training certifications, and many have written a couple of books. So with all of these common 'table-stakes' how are you going to differentiate yourself? *What is your Superpower?*

Creativity: *Talk the Language of Your Ideal Client*

Getting to know your ideal client *right down to their socks* was the next big lesson I learned. We all know how to identify the demographics of our ideal clients but how much do you really know about their deep aspirations and their true motivations? The more I learned to talk the actual language of my clients, the more successful I became. Today I can tell you that I work with women and men, aged 45-65 who want to explore 'what's next' as they start to become 'less-young'. Since not many people want to discuss aging in our youth-focused culture, I created this fun term to acknowledge this unique age and stage of life.

One way to learn a client's language is by carefully listening to what they *will say*, *won't say*, and *can't say*. As an example some of my clients, who are part of the 'sandwich generation', feel caught between work life and home life, caring for aging parents and bothersome boomerang kids, you know the ones that leave home and then move back. So here's what these clients will say; they feel pressure trying to *find some work-life balance*. What they won't say; *when will Junior finally move out of the house ... or why won't anyone else help me take care of Mom and Dad*. And what they can't say; *when will it be my turn to live life?* Being able to uncover and speak your clients deep motivational truths will demonstrate how you really understand their needs. This quickly develops trust and becomes new business.

I have learned that my ideal clients face many fears and uncertainty over late-career changes, retirement, bucket lists, becoming widowed or divorced, struggling as an empty nester, accepting the biodegradability of parenthood, and feeling sandwiched between aging parents and kids still at home. Writing and speaking *from experience* about the *headaches and heart-aches* in each of these scenarios shows that I understand the pain points of this group of people.

Please note that I deliberately used the word pain. People will always find money for aspirins and pain relief, while only a few will spend money on non-essential vitamins. Learn to speak about your ideal client's pain points and then tell them how your service will solve their problems. *How well do you really know your ideal clients pain points?*

Choice: *The Power Hour*

It can be a lot of fun defining your superpower and uncovering your clients' needs while building a business. The tougher part often comes trying to sign those clients up. Let's face it, great coaches don't always make great sales people and this is often the biggest struggle among solopreneurs. So here are two simple FREE activities which my business coach taught me to continually practice and when carried through they always make my business buzz

First, I was encouraged to build *a list of 100 people*. This included anyone close to my ideal client, who I could talk to about my service offerings. I started with former business consulting contacts, coaching colleagues, friends, and family. After talking to each prospect I would indicate on my list whether they *became a client* buying a service or were a potential *future client*. Occasionally they would fall into the category of never becoming a client.

At the end of *every* conversation, I would always ask if the person I was chatting with knew of anyone else that could benefit from my service. This has regularly been one way my list organically grows. Some other successful growth suggestions include; workshops, seminars, and personal development events. I do still employ the three foot rule and have gathered new clients while on wilderness treks, long-haul flights, and even at a funeral – so don't be shy, tell people about your superpower!

Secondly, the list of 100 people became the key for working the daily *power hour*. It is no secret that spending one hour every day can make a huge difference on anything, especially generating new sales. To be clear, I am not talking about emails, blogs, or social chats, what needed to happen was time to connect with each of those 100 people. Emails were just not as effectual as actually talking to a potential client. With a warm personable voice I could share how my services just might alleviate their pain while listening for objections.

Making the effort to talk to people was hard work. Not many of us truly like to cold call and yet I can truthfully say that everyone who diligently employs this practice inevitably enjoys a healthier and happier business life. Realistically not all of us can spare an hour every day. Personally I was quite happy when I spent two hours twice a week doing power hour activities. I scheduled the weekly time and when I disciplined myself to tenaciously complete the calls my business flourished. I can also say when I fell off the power hour wagon business invariably became quite sparse.

Choosing to do the *power hour* has been one of the most important FREE sales building activities that could make or break your business or practice. And I can truthfully share that doing these sales activities still requires a lot of my own *natural courage* to complete. *What choices are you making to grow your business?*

There are many differing ways to build a professional practice. I wouldn't hesitate to suggest reviewing some simple business building exercises found in any DIY section or site but the major key is taking the time for personal contact with your ideal clients.

I also strongly believe that to become a professional coach some professional training is required along with ongoing personal development. For me, Natural Courage has been an exciting evolutionary personal and professional journey. The three components of *clarity, creativity,* and *choice* have successfully been applied to changes in my life and business.

What heart-centered changes might you consider for your business? How or where can you find your own natural courage to make those changes?

Invaluable Reference:

Hanlon, Martha, and Chris Williams. *Customers Are the Answer to Everything: How to Get and Keep All the Customers Your Business Wants.* Garden City, NY: Morgan James Publishing, 2012.

Say*eda Habib, PCC*

Sayeda Habib, PCC is an author, speaker, and certified coach. Her passion and vision is to make coaching accessible to Muslims all over the globe. She appears on television, radio, runs webinars, and writes, all in order to educate the Muslim community about coaching, and how it can be used to help people create lives that they truly love.

Sayeda began her coaching career in 2004 and is certified as a Professional Certified Coach by the International Coach Federation. She is the author of "Discover the Best in You: Life Coaching for Muslims" She currently writes for a variety of Muslim publications and speaks at Islamic educational events and conferences.

CHAPTER 6

FIVE CRITICAL MISTAKES TO AVOID WHEN BUILDING A COACHING NICHE

Sayeda Habib, PCC

I was born and raised in Pakistan, and believe it or not, my first career was as a pastry chef. I was fulfilled doing what I was doing, and coaching wasn't something I'd heard of, as there was little awareness around it then. It is amazing how life leads you to where you need to be, even though you don't often plan things that way. I moved to the UK in 2000, due to some personal reasons, needing to rethink things. I began taking some courses in self-development, and a friend I'd made there suggested I give coaching a go. I was hungry to change things, so I began my own coaching journey then, but I didn't end up training as a coach until three years later. A lot happened during that time that led me to actually train as a coach.

The first, and most crucial thing was that I found that coaching actually worked for me. I was eager to do the work, and, with the support of my coach, I turned a lot of things around. Through my own coaching, I also realized that I was truly passionate about making a difference to other people. Actually, it's kind of in my blood. I come from a family of three generations of family who have been active in community service. I had always wanted to, but I wasn't sure of how I could transform my passion into a career. Things came together when I attended the Smart Marriages conference in the USA in 2003. I attended a session with ICF accredited coach, Patrick Williams. During the session, as luck would have it, I got the opportunity to coach Patrick during the practice, and he told me that I was "a natural." This was truly a turning point in my journey. I was already a believer in coaching, but that moment was a true "a-ha" moment for me. I was convinced that coaching was what I was truly made to do, and I haven't looked back since.

My core driving force is my passion to make a difference, but other ethics also come into play. For me, coaching is about giving my clients real value, always being honest about what I can, and can't offer, and giving support beyond the sessions. Another thing one of my teachers taught me, which has always stuck with me, is to be prepared for anything. He encouraged me to learn a whole lot of skills, and then leave them at the back of my mind when I'm with my clients. That way, I can be truly present with the client. When an intervention is needed, it just presents itself because I've learned it. I've always remembered this, and it's shaped my coaching over the years. Right from the beginning though, I was very clear that I wanted to get the best training possible so my training journey has been a long one. I still continue to sharpen my skills and learn new ones when opportunities arise.

When I started training, I didn't know the difference between a good course and a mediocre one. It turned out that the first course I completed left a lot to be desired. It was primarily self-study and practice groups. I learned that coaching is best learned with on-going face-to-face sessions and practice. Not to mention, you need a wide variety of skills, and some knowledge in various modalities. So after completing my first coaching diploma, I began widening my horizons. I studied NLP, and qualified as a practitioner, and then a Master Practitioner of NLP. I also qualified in NLP based hypnotherapy, Time Line Therapy, and have passed various other coaching courses over the years. Early on, I had already realized that coaching is not a regulated industry. I even saw some coaches doing things that made me cringe. So I had already decided that I would associate myself with the best coaching organization that I could find. This is when I decided that I wanted to be credentialed with the ICF. Erickson College, a Canadian organization, happened to be offering a full training in the UK. I took the opportunity to train with them, and after completing all the requirements I was awarded the Associate Coach Credential by the ICF in 2005. I later completed further requirements and was awarded the Professional Coach Certification as well. Since then, I've continued to develop my skills and keep my credential up to date.

I started my coaching practice by coaching friends and fellow students mostly. I guess that's how most coaches start out. After I qualified, I joined a few networking groups, and started going to the lunch and breakfast meetings. I would present myself as a life coach, for anyone who was looking to make changes in their lives. I would often come back from these meetings feeling disheartened. I was coaching a client or two, but nothing substantial was coming my way. I later realized that people weren't "getting" me, or what I was offering. Why would they connect to a Muslim woman wearing hijab? After all, I was an alien being to most of them, and they would be right now to choose me. I didn't know what it was like to be male banker or lawyer working in the heart of London. There was no rapport there. I began realizing that I was wasting my time. I understood that I had to build a niche for my practice.

One of the most important things you can do when building a practice is to focus in on a powerful niche right in the beginning. Not only will this focus your own efforts but it will set you apart from all the "noise." You will find fulfilment, and be able to distinguish yourself as an expert. There are several good reasons to build a niche, however, there are 5 critical mistakes that are best avoided when doing so. I learned what these mistakes are from my own experiences, as I didn't have anyone mentoring me. There weren't any Muslim coaches out there when I started, so I was navigating on my own. Be aware of these mistakes, and take the recommended actions instead. You will find these steps helpful in building a strong niche and a successful practice. Good luck!

Mistake 1: Being vague about your niche
The first critical mistake was that I was vague about my niche. I was nervous to limit myself, worrying about where clients would come from. Whatever the reason, being vague about your niche sends prospective clients a wishy-washy message. They aren't sure about whether you can help them or not, so the enquiries you will get will be half-hearted at best. You will sound unclear and come across as unreliable. You will lose extra time trying to convert these clients into actual customers. Having a clear niche helps you attract genuine clients who really want the help that you can offer them.

Action to take: Identify your niche early
The clearer you are about your niche, the more likely you are to build a

strong practice. It is critical that your niche is very clear and obvious. If your niche isn't quite clear in your mind, then begin with focusing in on yourself. Reflect on your own coaching journey, what you gained from it, and how it inspired you. Ask people in your community about important issues that would draw them towards coaching. Another way to proceed is to choose one or two areas that you feel you can AUTHENTICALLY work in. These will be areas that you have some knowledge of such as specific life experiences, your culture, or faith. The more authentic you are, the more chances of success you have in your practice. You may have a nagging fear that you are limiting yourself, but you actually aren't. You are setting up a more clear and focused practice going ahead. If you can meet people and clearly tell them what it is you do, and who you serve, then they will remember that, and forward your message on with that much clarity. Help others to help you promote your business. Choose website domain names, and tag lines that demonstrate your niche clearly, or come as close to your message as possible.

Mistake 2: Creating a product that's too broad
An e-book, CD, or course can be a powerful tool for your practice. However, if your product is too vague, then chances are that your niche may not immediately latch on to how the product relates to them. My first product didn't directly appeal to the Muslim market. My target audience didn't see the appeal, and so I had a thousand CD's that I had to get rid of. Granted, things are digital now, however, having a product that doesn't scream to your target market will be wasted time and effort on your part.

Action to take: Create a product that specifically appeals to your niche.
You may be in a hurry to get something out there, but don't be. Planning is essential here. Create a free report, course, or audio program that meets a need of your target market. It's ok to be specific and hone in on one or two things. Avoid giving away too much. Think about the talents you have and how you can capitalize on them. If you can write, then a book or articles may be the way. If you are better at relating face to face, then consider a video course. Your product should grab the attention of your target market. Buyers should be able to ask the question "is this for me or not?" and know immediately. It should do what it says on the tin, and also deliver value that helps the consumer understand your service

better. Whether you choose to sell the product, or give it for fr[ee is] a choice you can make depending on your own goals.

Once you've planned out the product, then the rest of the steps will become much easier. There are a number of services available to help you create your product with relatively little expense. Be creative, and get help where you need it.

Mistake 3: Not being choosy about your clients
Have you been fearful or concerned about where your clients will come from? I certainly was, especially in the beginning. Another mistake is taking on clients that aren't a good fit for your niche, aren't able to pay your fee, or aren't really ready for coaching to begin with. If you find yourself trying to convince someone to try coaching, or lowering your prices to a point that you're not comfortable, I urge you to refrain from doing so. I, unfortunately, have experience in this area. When I began coaching, it was hardly heard of in the Muslim community. I would get enquiries from people who weren't really sure what coaching was, or they wanted help but didn't see value in making the financial investment. I wound up compromising on my fee, or trying to convince them to give it a try. I have to say that this was unsuccessful each and every time it happened. Clients are either willing to invest in coaching or they're not! It takes an intuitive coach to be able to decipher that. The more experience you gain, the faster you will be able to glean who is ready and who isn't. I well appreciate the fear of not knowing where the next client will come from, but compromising in this way doesn't get the results, so why do it.

Action to take: Be proactive in building good relationships
The best way to combat fear is to allow it to be there, and shift your focus towards what's in your control. Start building good relationships within your niche. Find some organisations and key people within your niche that would be able to get the word out. Offer them a free workshop, or one or two free coaching sessions. This could be a well thought-through strategy to promote yourself within your niche.

Building good relationships will build your confidence. If key organizations or individuals promote you, then that will also build your reputation as an expert. You will begin to create ambassadors who will promote you and your work. To do this effectively, you will need to maintain your reputation, so be clear about your own business values and ensure you practice them. Be open to receiving feedback, and ask people to give it in written form whenever possible. Start collecting testimonials from key people in your niche, and you can use them on your marketing material. Remember, if these are key personalities, then your prospective clients will know who they are. Be clear about what you are offering, stick to that, and offer your clients value. If your clients have positive experiences, they will be likely to refer you on. Do keep in mind that each niche works differently, so request referrals only when appropriate.

4th Mistake: Approaching all publicity as good publicity.
It is sometimes thought that all publicity is good publicity, but this isn't true in the coaching business. You are in the business of helping people, so a negative review is hardly helpful. Negative, or incorrect publicity will go against you, and things tend to stick these days due to social media. People Google any professional service they engage, so if they find a negative review or article, they will go and find another coach.

For example, I once went on a T.V. program with a presenter who didn't really understand what coaching is. I had met with her, and had a long chat the day before the show she still hadn't quite grasped the concept. On that live TV show, she had myself and another guest on the show. The lady was supposed to be someone who was also in a helping profession, but as I found out on the show, she had a completely different agenda to mine. She was aggressive, and it totally negated anything that I was trying to say. I had family and friends watching the show and they said that it didn't look good. This was one of my first experiences with the media, and a great learning experience it was. That show was the most effort I've made for a show, and yet it backfired. All because I didn't ask about the other guests, and even though, I wasn't convinced about the presenter, I turned against my instincts and went ahead. I've been on several television shows since then, but I research in what the show is about, any other guests, and what we will be talking about. There have been times when it's not felt right and I'm no longer afraid to turn these down. I've learned that every opportunity in the media isn't always a good one.

Action to take: Make smart use of the media to build your brand.
Making careful use of the media can provide huge leverage to your business. This includes all forms of media including radio, television, print and online media. Ensure that you choose media that your niche is plugged into. Think about certain times when your niche may be more willing to engage with your message and start preparing in advance. Research any publications or television channels that you intend to approach. Get to know them, so that you can choose if they are good fit, and how to best approach them so that your message is heard. Use news events to get your message across as well. Another thing to be mindful of is where and how you are participating on online media. Refrain from any pages, groups or websites that may be out of alignment with your niche. If you are seen as having opposing sets of personal values, this will ultimately go against your business. I have written for various publications over the years, and I ensure that none of them carry viewpoints that would be in direct opposition to my own personal and professional values. This is how you build your reputation, by using the media wisely and always being in alignment with your values.

Mistake 5: Trying to hold onto clients
You are putting in so much work so of course you'll want things to go the way you'd planned. This is all fine, except when you're attached to the results. This primarily shows up for coaches when clients want to leave. The coach will do whatever he or she can to "get" the client to stay on. This is a mistake. Coaching only works when clients are fully vested in the process, so its pointless trying to convince clients to stay. Allow the client to make his own choice, and if you leave the process gracefully, they may well come back when the need arises. I've had quite a few clients over the years who've completed their coaching and then contacted me years later for some follow up coaching.

Action to take: Let go and Take action.
Combat the temptation to "hold on" to clients by providing them with lasting value. Even if they have one session with you, and it is a powerful session, they will tend to remember it for a long time. Once they want to go, just let go. Use the time available to work "on" your business consistently. Create products as a first step. Be ready with some workshops, or talks, so you are ready to step in as the chance arrives. Remember opportunities favour those who are prepared to take them.

Sow several seeds, and then focus in on the ones that begin to sprout. The right clients will indeed find you- if you are available to be found! I wish you the best in establishing a successful coaching business, one that is fulfilling for you, and transformational for your clients.

Wendy L. Yost

Wendy L. Yost partners with individuals, small businesses, Fortune 500 companies and non-profit and educational organizations to grow through change and generate results. With a Master's Degree in Leadership, several coaching certifications and a comprehensive list of speaking topics, Wendy passionately illuminates spiritual principles in ways that leave people inspired to take action. A recent example includes her 2016 TEDx Talk on Learning to Listen to Your Life, So You Can Lead it. As a published writer, Wendy contributed the chapter The Art of Cultivating Professional References for 101 Great Ways to Enhance Your Career by Michelle & David Riklan and serves as a Featured Author for http://simplereminders.com/, imparting coaching principles through stories for the community's seven million+ subscribers. Wendy is working on two books: One to help children and their parents trust their intuition and another to help female holistic practitioners grow their businesses, while navigating divorce. Wendy leads monthly events in Los Angeles every New and Full Moon weaving her love of nature and ritual with ancient wisdom.

Wendy can be reached at (818) 660-MORE [Pacific Standard Time] and via www.moreisavailable.com

CHAPTER 7

MARKETING YOUR COACHING SERVICES TO LOCAL COLLEGES AND UNIVERSITIES

Wendy L. Yost

Think about where you live. Now, think about how many colleges and universities exist within an hour or two of your house. Did you think of the different kinds of colleges and universities there might be? For example in California, we have public schools (those in the University of California system, those in the California State University system, those in the Community College system and Trade Schools) as well as private schools. Using the map feature on my smart phone, and entering the search terms, "college" and then "university", I learned that there are nearly 20 colleges and universities less than an hour from my house. I don't know about you, but with all that is involved with booking flights and managing hotel accommodations, I enjoy working with local clients. And I really enjoy working with local clients who I can develop a relationship with over time, receive referrals from, plan ahead to meet their evolving needs and who serve a population who, by design, graduate and are replaced with a new population needing my programs and services about every four years.

Over the last 20 years I have held positions within three of the four divisions that comprise most universities: Academic Affairs, Student Affairs and University Advancement. This has afforded me an interesting vantage point of the many facets involved in student success, and has provided tremendous insight into which areas of campus tend to invest in personal services to meet their desired objectives. This is really useful to know, given I left my full time career in Higher Education back in 2007, to dedicate more time and attention to my coaching and consulting practice. And since then have been employed by over one hundred departments on college and university campuses to provide skill building and personal development workshops, to coach employees, to mentor faculty, and to assist administrators with the many complexities involved with organizational change.

In addition to operating my coaching and consulting business, since 2007 I have served as a part time member of the adjunct faculty at California State University, Northridge. During that time I have taught a Leadership class for 25 semesters, along with a rotation of the following classes: Marketing, Entrepreneurialism, Event Planning, Non-Profit Management & Fund Development, Women & Leisure and Play & Human Potential. In 2014, I was honored with a Distinguished Teaching Award and the Leadership class that I teach was voted "Best Class on Campus" by students through the university's campus newspaper. In short, I have a rich history of working with college students, faculty, staff and administrators, and I want to share what I have learned in service to your sharing your gifts and talents on the campuses near you.

In this chapter, I will provide an overview of possible points of entry; provide information on where to look for additional information specific to campuses in your area; share details on related professional associations; speak to the ethical considerations involved with working with this client base; dispel a few myths and misconceptions; and offer up a series of examples to give you a sense of what is involved with partnering with a college or university campus.

In order to get you thinking specifically about what kind of opportunities might exist for you, I want you to call to mind your favorite programs and services to offer, and then review the list below to see where, on a typical college or university, your programs and services might be a good fit.

Issues Campuses Invest Heavily in Addressing
- Bullying
- Depression
- Eating Disorders
- Financial Literacy (Student Debt)

- Hazing
- Sexual Assault
- Substance Abuse
- Suicide
- Smoking Cessation

Specific Populations that Campuses Invest in Serving
- Freshman
- International Students
- Student Veterans
- Students with Disabilities
- Transfer Students
- Underrepresented Students
- Underserved Students

Sampling of Academic Departments that Bring Guest Lecturers to Campus:
- Africana Studies
- American Indian Studies
- Asian American Studies
- Central American Studies
- Chicana/o Studies
- College of Extended Learning / Open University / Extension
- Gender and Women's Studies
- Jewish Studies
- Lesbian, Gay, Bisexual and Transgender (LGBT) / Queer Studies
- Mexican-American Studies
- Middle Eastern and Islamic Studies
- Pan-African Studies
- Religious Studies

Student-Focused Departments that Hire Speakers, Coaches and Consultants:
Given different departments go by different names on different campuses, the list below includes possible iterations.

- Alumni Relations
- Associated Students / Student Government
- Athletic Department / Intercollegiate Athletics

- Campus Activities / Student Involvement / Student Development
- Campus Ministries / Interfaith Council
- Career Center
- Clubs & Organizations / Student Organizations
- Counseling Services
- Disabilities Resources
- Emerging Leaders / Leadership Institute / Student Leadership
- Greek Life: Fraternities and Sororities
- Health Center
- International Student Center / Study Abroad Center / Exchange Student Center
- Lesbian, Gay, Bisexual, Transgender (LGBT) Center / Pride Center
- Orientation / New Student Orientation / Transfer Student Orientation
- Student Housing
- Student Union
- Veterans Resource Center

Faculty and Staff-Focused Departments that Hire Speakers, Coaches and Consultants:

- Employee Assistance
- Equity and Diversity
- Faculty Development
- New Faculty Orientation
- Professional Development / Training and Development

List of Common Training Topics

- Conflict Resolution
- Creative Marketing
- Diversity
- Emotional Intelligence
- Employability Skills
- Ethics
- Free Speech
- Fundraising
- Goal Setting

- New Supervisors
- Peer Student Leadership
- Recognition
- Retaining Members
- Self Advocacy
- Social Media
- Strategic Planning/Vision/Mission
- Student Employee Management
- Student Organization Management
- Students Supervising Students
- Sustainability
- Wellness

Visit www.moreisavailable.com/CoachingCodeBonus for a list of commemorative months and days that campuses consider when booking speakers.

Based on the many items above, what caught your attention, and left you thinking, I could help with that? If you haven't already done so, feel free to put a check by those items. Next you will want to do some basic research on the campuses that you are wanting to reach out to. The easiest way to do that is to visit the college or university's web site and go on a campus tour. There are several quick and easy ways to gather information and insights into your intended audience online, the trick is knowing where to look. College and university web sites typically involve hundreds, if not thousands of individual pages. So your first desired destination to locate is their "A-Z page" which is an alphabetical listing of departments, programs, organizations, and facilities. That is a good site to bookmark for each campus you are interested in reaching out to.

Once you are on the A-Z page, there are three places to look for concise information about the campus that you are researching: The Home Page, the page for Institutional Research and the page for the President's Office. Each of these pages contain overviews on the things like the college or university's mission, vision and values; a snapshot of student, faculty and staff demographics and past speeches that the president has delivered that speak to current priorities. The A-Z page will also be helpful in determining information on things like locating a Campus

Map, scheduling a Campus Tour, and what you need to know about Parking, given each will likely be listed under those names.

Also on the A-Z page, you can find things like Academic Year Calendars, the Course Catalog and the Experts Directory. Academic Calendars are helpful because they will tell you whether the campus is on Semesters or Quarters, when classes are in session and which holidays the campus recognizes (and will be closed on). Given the need to have each semester or quarter contain a set amount of weeks, some campuses celebrate holidays on days other than the official date. The Course Catalog is helpful in that it typically includes a list of Majors and Minors that students can study, which could lead to classes that are of interest to you to serve as a Guest Lecturer for. Serving as a Guest Lecturer is a great way to get your foot in the door on a college or university campus, and to see if working with college students is something that you enjoy. As an Adjunct Faculty Member I bring in roughly two Guest Lecturers for each of the classes I teach each semester, to help ensure that I am able to meet all of the Learning Outcomes for the course, and to expose the students to local professionals who might assist them in making connections off campus, through professional networking opportunities, internships and jobs.

As we wrap up all that is available through the A-Z page on a campus' web site, it is also worth noting that in addition to serving as a coach, speaker or consultant on a college or university campus, you might also want to consider using their Campus Newspaper, Radio Station or Bookstore to promote your programs and services. While most campuses are moving to a weekly or quarterly printed copy of their newspaper and maintaining the rest of the news online, they do tend to have a solid handle on using social media to get the word out about topics of note. So you might want to consider visiting their web page to see what the rates are for running an ad in their print and online media. The campus radio station might be another desirable promotional option, depending on their listening audience and how well it overlaps with the clients you typically serve. There might also be opportunities to serve as a guest expert on a live radio show, something I volunteered my time for at a local university, after learning that they record the shows live, and then archive them on the radio stations web site and their YouTube channel. Making it something that I can easily share with prospective clients, that I didn't have to pay to produce, edit, engineer or upload.

Friendly Tip: Getting on Campus for Under $100

There are two things that you can do to promote your programs and services that are relatively quick, relatively easy and relatively inexpensive. And both tend to be housed within a college or university's Student Union.

Most campuses have a public location where Clubs & Organizations Mail Boxes reside. And anyone is welcome to put flyers or brochures into the mailboxes. Not all clubs check their mailboxes boxes regularly, and not all of the information actually gets shared with the organization's members. Yet it is free and so it is worth considering, given your only expense would be the copies or brochures. Another way to use this opportunity is to visit the mailboxes, note which student organizations catch your eye based on shared characteristics or overlapping interests and then ask the staff members nearby about the best way to contact the President or Advisor for select student organizations. Doing so could allow you to reach out to them in a more direct way.

The second way to inexpensively promote your programs or services on campus is by renting a table in the University Student Union or in the quad area of campus. Setting up a table and finding unique ways to engage students during the noon time lunch rush can lead to opportunities to speak at Greek Life meetings, trainings that Student Athletes attend and meetings held by student clubs and organizations. Costs vary depending on the size of the campus, the location of the table and the duration of your stay. Yet typically involve an investment of under $100. This opportunity can be maximized by booking a date that a noontime concert or other campus event is also scheduled.

Having taken you on what may feel like the equivalent of a campus tour, I now want to move off campus to the professional associations. There are a number of professional associations that colleges and universities belong to, and related local, regional and national conferences that campuses invest in sending staff to. Below is a list of all of the professional associations that I was aware of through my own involvement and that of colleagues I worked with during my time in Student Affairs. I encourage you visit the web sites provided and see if there are any local or regional conferences coming up that you could submit a program proposal for. The advantage of doing so is exposure to the campuses in your area, with the people who make the decisions about who to bring to campus. In addition, at some of these conferences, NACA most predominantly, showcases of possible speakers are included in the conference agenda and systems are in place to support campuses in working with colleagues on campuses in their area to "Block Book" speakers, to reduce costs.

American College Personnel Association (ACPA)
http://www.myacpa.org/

American Student Government Association (ASGA)
http://www.asgaonline.com

Associations of College Unions International (ACUI)
http://www.acui.org/

National Association of Student Personnel Administrators (NASPA)
https://www.naspa.org/

National Association of Campus Activities (NACA)
https://www.naca.org

National Orientation Directors Association (NODA)
http://www.nodaweb.org/

According to the NACA web site, "Block Booking is when three or more schools work together with Associates in the booking process to coordinate days and times, maximizing routing for a given act or performer. In return for this convenient routing and multiple contracts, the Associate Member agrees to perform each date for a discounted rate, saving each participating campus money. Usually, the more schools participating in a block, the deeper the discount to each campus."

In addition to speaking opportunities at these professional conferences, most conferences also have Expos or Vendor Fairs where you can purchase a table or booth to share information about your programs or services, and the conference coordinators are typically looking for sponsors to provide a wide range of items needed for the conference, including items that are provided for each conference attendee.

In some cases, in order to able to speak at a conference, you need to be an Associate Member of the organization, so you will want to weigh whether or not that expenses is worth the investment, depending on the volume of work you are interested in doing with colleges and universities. An advantage to doing so is that you typically get access to a directory of member schools as part of your membership.

As you consider the different ways you might engage with colleges and universities near you, it is also important to consider how you engage with them. At the time of this printing, the coaching industry isn't regulated in the United States, and there is not a single governing body providing coaching certifications. That, in conjunction with having earned multiple coaching and spiritual counseling certifications from a wide range of certification programs, has required that I choose a central approach to ethics to align with. For me, that is the International Coaching Federation's (ICF) Code of Ethics. The ICF has been monitoring trends in the industry for 20+ years and provides a comprehensive list of ethical considerations on their web site that is adopted by its Board of Directors at regular intervals. Some of the items listed in the ICF Code of Ethics[1] of particular note when working in partnership with colleges and universities include:

- Refrain from unlawful discrimination in occupational activities, including age, race, gender orientation, ethnicity, sexual orientation, religion, national origin or disability.
- Recognize and honor the efforts and contributions of others and only claim ownership of my own material. I understand that violating this standard may leave me subject to legal remedy by a third party.
- Maintain, store and dispose of any records, including electronic files and communications, created during my coaching engagements in a manner that promotes confidentiality, security and privacy and complies with any applicable laws and agreements.
- Hold responsibility for being aware of and setting clear, appropriate and culturally sensitive boundaries that govern interactions, physical

or otherwise, I may have with my clients or sponsor(s).
- Avoid any sexual or romantic relationship with current clients or sponsor(s) or students, mentees or supervisees.

[1] As adopted by the Board of Directors in June 2015, and as shared on the organization's web site as of August 2016.

In addition to aligning my approach to ethics with the ICF Code of Ethics, I also make a point of visiting the Mission, Vision and Values page of any college or university I consider partnering with, so that I can ensure that I will be willing and able to function at my best as a coach, speaker and consultant. This helps me write key words and phrases into my communications and proposals to demonstrate alignment. And it also helps me determine when a campus might be less of an easy fit given my style and approach. As an example, upon conducting research on a local Jesuit University, I quickly realized that given I openly use examples that honor all religious traditions and I am a long-standing ally to the Lesbian, Gay, Bisexual and Transgender (LGBT) community, and by design build inclusive language into my work and any written materials I create to support desired outcomes, that I probably should pass on proposing my services to that particular campus or any of the campuses represented by the Association of Jesuit Colleges and Universities (AJCU). On the flip side, if you review the list on the above association's web site and feel a deep kinship for working with campuses that share your ideals, then you now have another list of possible campuses to reach out to.

Time to dispel a myth. Many people think that colleges and universities don't have money. While it is true that most colleges and universities are underfunded in a variety of ways, money does exist for what university administrators refer to as "co-curricular learning". This usually takes the form of the campus bringing in a speaker or coach to meet with a group of students to achieve a particular "learning outcome". These learning outcomes are critical, because they are what justify the expense, and allow the program being offered to be measure for effectives, which influences future funding for similar events.

If your head is already spinning, here's a simple way to translate something you likely already do for potential clients into university speak: Convert what you are already using as indicators of benefits of working with you and testimonials from clients into learning outcomes.

Learning outcomes are basically what students will be able to do, know or understand as a result of working with you. And, if further clarity would be helpful, a quick search for something like, "student learning outcomes, communication" will provide a host of possible examples you can adapt.

Another way that you can speak to learning outcomes is by looking at the latest research on what employers want students to learn in college. Bill Coplin wrote a book on this subject that was revised in 2012 and will likely be revised again. And StrengthsFinder 2.0 by Tom Rath and Now Discover Your Strengths by Marcus Buckingham and Donald O. Clifton are additional book that colleges and universities use to help students articulate their strengths in ways that matter to potential employers.

A key consideration when offering your services to a local college or university is to know your audience. The easiest way to do this is to visit the school's web site, then visit their online campus directory, and look up the following: Institutional Research. Institutional Research is where all of the data is archived for students, faculty and staff on that campus. I am no stranger to borrowing language from a campus' Institutional Research page to help my proposal stand out from the rest. When an administrator sits down to review information received from possible vendors, those that quickly rise to the top are the ones where the vendor took the time to personalize their communication making it specific to the needs of their campus, using key words and phrases that are quick to catch their attention. Words and phrases like, "Factors Affecting the Success of Freshmen", referencing how the program you offer fits into the National Survey of Student Engagement, providing testimonials from college students who reference how your program or service helped reduce stress or from administrators sharing how naturally your program supported their learning outcomes.

As with learning anything new, Higher Education comes with its own vocabulary. So in effort to give you a sense of the kinds of words that demonstrate you know what your are doing, and you know how to do it on a college or university campus, here is a sampling:

- Academic Standing
- Accommodations
- CAS Standards
- Conditionally Admitted Students
- Continuation Rates

- Core Curriculum
- Critical Thinking Across the Disciplines
- Curriculum
- E-learning
- Family Education Rights and Privacy Act (FERPA)
- General Education
- Graduate
- Graduation
- Learning Habits
- Learning Outcomes
- Matriculate
- Non-Traditional Students
- Orientation
- Persistence
- Program Assessment
- Retention
- Satisfactory Academic Progress (SAP)
- Sophomore Slump
- Student Engagement
- Student Success
- Sustainability
- The Dream Act
- Title V.
- Undeclared
- Undergraduate
- Underserved Population

I encourage you to do a quick search for "Higher Education, [insert term above]" for any of the terms above that you are unfamiliar with or curious about. And know that this list is in no way exhaustive. While I have 20+ years of experience in Higher Education, one thing I know for sure is that new theories, new trends and new terminology are always being added to the discourse. So even I sometimes have to look something up to remain current!

I'm guessing that by now it's clear how passionate I am about working with colleges and universities. It's true. I am! And, I am convinced that I would not have made it through school were it not for co-curricular activities. In Grade School it was Girl Scouts, in High School it was Yearbook and helping the School Nurse with a Blood Drive, in college it was being an Orientation Leader, Yearbook (again!), Peer Minister, Peer Counselor, Resident Advisor, Student Senator, University Ambassador, Sorority Member, Residence Hall Association President and Sorority President. When I think about what eventually had me become a coach, it was what I learned through each of those experiences and through the themes woven through all of them. There will always be students like me, who are more interested in learning that takes place outside the classroom, than the learning that takes place inside the classroom, and we need coaches like you helping them learn the skills they need to succeed while also showing them that they can make a career out of doing what they love most.

So start anywhere on any of the lists provided. Perhaps reach out to your own alma mater. See where their needs meet your interests, and how you might partner to serve the students, the faculty and/or the staff, while adding an organizational client to your list and the potential for a lot of on campus referrals. My favorite part of working as a coach, speaker and consultant on campus, is when a student who you worked with many years ago, ends up in a role where they are the hiring authority charged to bring in a coach, speaker and consultant, and they think back to the person who made a difference for them so many years ago, and they track you down and you get to work with each other again.

May marketing your coaching services to local colleges and universities lead to many such conversations for you!

Tim Johnson

Tim Johnson is a success coach who helps people get business results and personal fulfilment. Tim has a demonstrable track record in the entrepreneurial space having built not one but two multimillion dollar businesses (both over $5m turnover) from start up. But he has also experienced significant setbacks, losing his arm in a car crash and relationship breakdowns both personally and in business.

With an MBA and an engineering degree Tim has a passion for discovering how things work and how to make them scale. Working through his challenging experiences Tim has dug deep and studied diverse spiritual approaches. He has packaged the wisdom in a practical and accessible ways to enable personal and business growth for people searching greater meaning and success in their lives.

Tim is also author of The Success Book – how to grow yourself and your business, published by LID publishing.

www.meaningfulsuccess.co.uk

CHAPTER 8

A TRULY SUCCESSFUL AND SUSTAINABLE BUSINESS MODEL FOR COACHES.

Tim Johnson

My name is Tim Johnson and I've developed the Meaningful Success Coaching Program for business owners, leaders and managers. Meaningful Success helps shift the perspectives of business owners along with "how to" training and mentoring to deliver business results AND personal fulfilment.

My story in short. I was successful in business, had the standard shields of success, had a car accident, lost my arm and was forced out of my business. I had to start all over and went to co-found another successful business. But when everything unravelled I went on a 2 year journey in search of making sense of it all. I spent time with lots of schools of wisdom, who all thought they had the answer. My view is they all have part of the answer and combining it all with a simple model to navigate is my way of creating meaning and sharing a practical way forward.

There is often the perception that there is a trade-off between doing meaningful work and producing financial results. This can manifest in people feel they have to endure an environment where the behaviours and values are not what they are entirely comfortable with, they do activities they'd rather not and make decisions to suit the organisation's (usually short term) aims that at odds with their personal values. But this is all accepted as "that's business" that's just the way it is. Over time this can cause undue stress, with knock on effects on business performance, health and life at home.

The reverse idea that some hold, particularly in the alternative health and wellness sector, people often feel they would be selling their soul if they got commercial, that it's wrong to make lots of money, as money is the root of all evil – but this is simply not the case. For the people that put a high emphasis on meaning in their work, the more commercially successful they can make their business, the more people they reach and influence with their good works. The more commercial successful the more can be reinvested in developing the product or service and to scale up the delivery. Even if a fully scaled up business is not the priority the extra money created from commercial success could be used to support charitable organisations and do more good there too for example.

We live in a celebrity society where we are conditioned to aspire to fame and fortune, or wealth and status for mere mortals. That success is out there, when, an external future orientated state. And this causes much suffering.

However despite going through a journey of losing it all, learning to reduce my attachment to the things I previously held dear, being comfortable in your own skin regardless of external circumstances isn't the holy grail in itself because we still have to interact with the everyday concerns of western living. So I had a dilemma, if success isn't out there when we externally create stuff, and it's not right here right now when I connect with myself where is it?

This is when I created a simple model to make sense of this apparent paradox.

We are conditioned to believe that external circumstances are where to find success, fame and fortune, wealth and status, great relationships and fantastic children. When we have these, then we will feel better. I played this game, and did pretty well at it. But no matter how well I played it, it didn't mask the underlying feeling of inadequacy inside. Despite having an engineering degree, an MBA, a trained mediator, training in tax, insolvency, sales, speaking, read hundreds of books and attended endless courses, communities and seminars. I couldn't knowledge myself into adequacy, I couldn't collect houses cars and holidays to prove my adequacy, I couldn't meditate, run or drink myself into adequacy.

What I learnt is that there are two worlds, an inner world and an outer world. That looking for the outer world to make us feel great is effectively outsourcing our happiness to external people and circumstances, and on a practical level that's simply not a good strategy. So we need to take care, control and ownership of inner world, the world of personal responsibility, where we become more able to choose our responses to external stimuli, to be able to choose how we'd like to become as people, and to choose to be more generous with our spirit.

But we don't live in an internal world, the reality is we live in a messy complicated messed up world with all sorts of crazy, magical, awful and dull stuff happening. The key is not being blissfully self-contained meditating on a mountain top, it's taking control of yourself to better interact with the outside world.

There are two key fundamental necessities as human beings, without which it is difficult to have a sense of meaning, and these are connection and creation. We are social animals and without connection we wither on the vine, in tribal times being evicted from the tribe would almost certainly lead to death. Connection is a hard wired necessity. The other fundamental is creation. We have an in-built to create, to make stuff happen, to contribute, to give back in some way shape or form, whether that's being an architect or hairdresser it's providing some form of service to others whether it is paid for or not.

When you map out these two necessities with the two worlds it looks like this:-

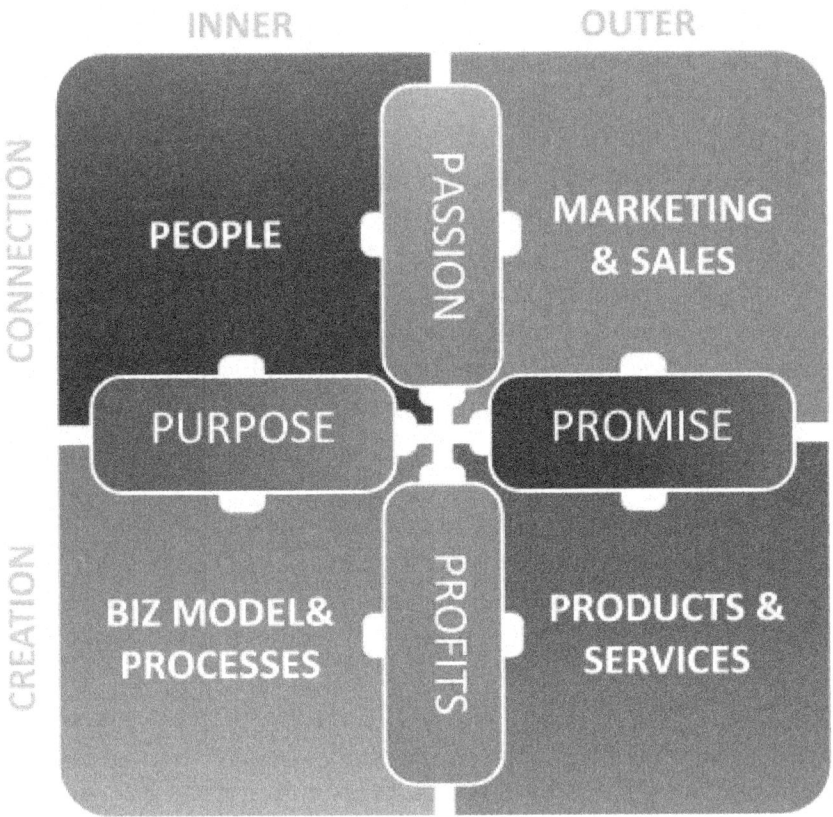

Where the Outer Creation is the world of work where we create out money. This is rational logical, Newtonian physics based world, where we reside in our heads.

The Outer Connection is the world of people and relationships. This is the heart based realm.

The Inner Connection is the connection we have with ourselves. This is the inner peace and stillness realm. This is our soul connection.

And the Inner Creation is the domain of intent, the way we want to be, the things we want to do and the things we want to have. This is the realm of dreaming and imagination, the law of attraction and quantum mechanics.

There are 4 connectors of Authenticity, Appreciation, Culture and Vision that link the quadrants together:-

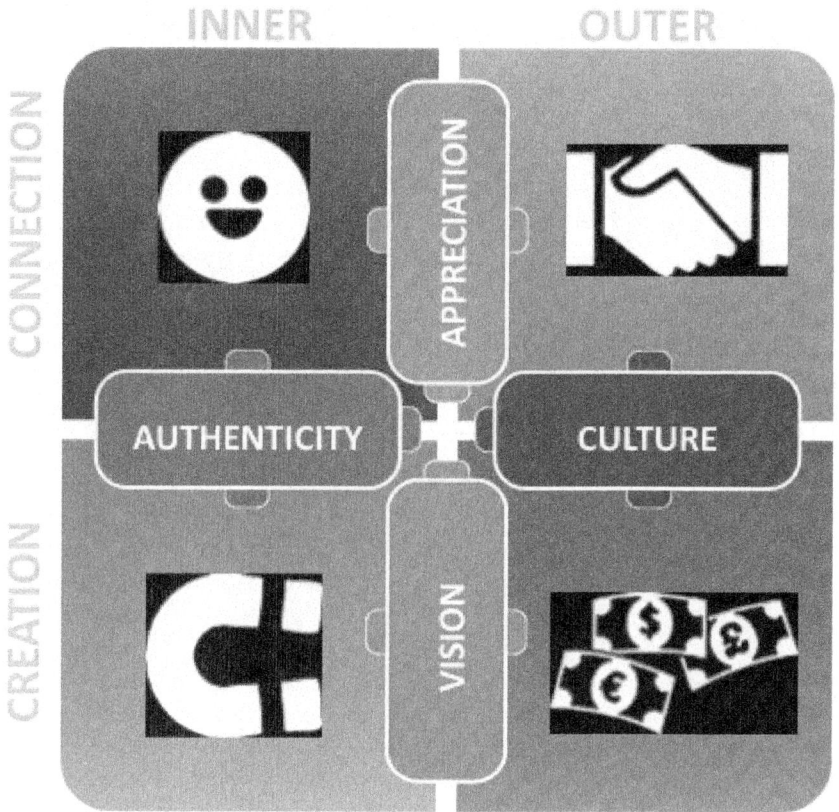

And then the whole model is fractal or holonic, so we can zoom into the work quadrant and look at business strategy through this lens:-

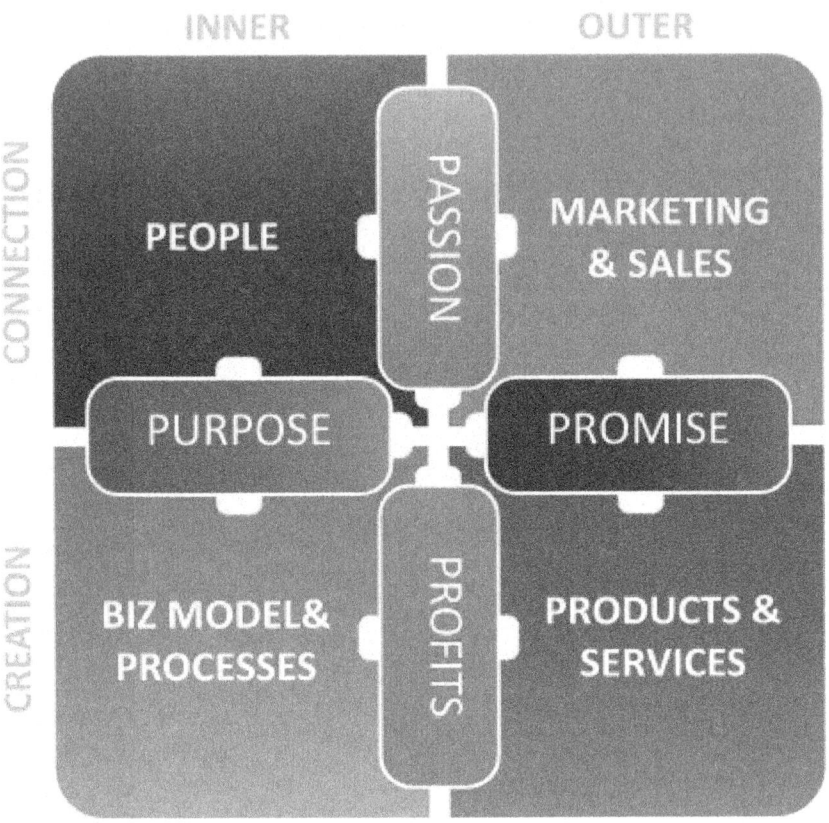

Where through connecting Purpose, Passion and Promise with the 4 core quadrants of the business the profits will flow.

The bottle neck of any business is at the top, so grow the business it is also necessary to grow the business leaders. Working with these 2 models in tandem in conjunction with their sub-models allows significant positive change to be enabled.

Typically the 3 core issues that this work can help address are

1. My business is running me: I'm giving it my all, I'm juggling all the

balls, spinning all the plates, and making things happen. Sure it's exciting and rewarding but I just can't see myself letting go of the reins enough to ease back a little as it's bound to fall apart without me pushing so hard. Is there a way round this?

2. Is this it? I thought by now I'd be much happier with my life, but instead my business has turned into a job that I can't move on from. I feel stuck, unmotivated and in a rut. How did it get like this is there realistically anything that can be done about it?

3. My business is going great – but the rest of my life? Less so!

So you want to be a coach?

The good news is that it's a truly intrinsically rewarding experience to help enable and encourage someone to transform their lives and their business and to get paid for the privilege. The less good news is that it's a crowded marketplace and whilst undoubtedly there are a lot of coaches who do great work and create great businesses, the reality is the bulk of people who set out to be coaches don't make a successful business out of it and land out going back into employment or different opportunity, although with the added skillset of coaching training.

There are some fundamental questions to consider as you think about the road ahead:-

Do you want to go it alone? Or under the banner of an established organisation.

My personal story in the coaching arena can be illuminating

15 years ago I'd sold the shares in the business I'd successfully taken from $250,000 a year to $6million a year turnover with a staff of 50 and state of the art manufacturing facilities, and took an MBA. I had the practical experience and the academic qualifications to go with it, so I had significant credibility. But I found when I tried to market myself as a one-man-band management consultant, gaining traction in the

marketplace was difficult because I didn't have a set process and tools to productise my knowledge. Having these would have made it easier to explain the value I'd be able to deliver.

A potential introducer of business, an accountant, suggested to me that I'd better working with an established organisation has they had an established brand and the backing of team support structure.

I took the advice and enrolled with the recommend firm. Their model was no up front franchise or license fee, but that I paid for the ongoing training, and shared revenue on 50/50 basis. In return I got to use their IP (intellectual property – that is there models and processes) and got the support of the local regional team leader. The challenge was that their fee structure was so high that only conversation at the group training events for coaches, was "have you got any new clients lately?' – most had not.

Recognising that the vast majority of coaches were failing to create a sustainable business for themselves I reasoned that I'd be better off creating my own niche brand and setting out that way. So I established a business brand called Business Mediation – combining conflict management and business strategy to unlock dysfunctional boards of directors and effect business turnaround that way. However the niche was too narrow, dysfunctional boards tend not to admit they have the problem, and when it becomes apparent the existing accountants and lawyers tend to draw out the dispute and create healthy fees for themselves. So whilst there was clearly a market need, there was not market demand.

There is another well-known global business coaching franchise that happily recruits consultants as long as they have a cheque book and a pulse. There is a high up-front fee, and expected marketing fund, and a 7 year contract for monthly fees to stay in the organisation. Many fail because as coming from backgrounds such as teaching or being in the fire-service doesn't give them the credibility to be a business coach, no matter how good the training. You need to have been there and done it too, to be able to really understand the nuances and difficulties, otherwise we all could simply read the manual and be sorted.

I subsequently took out a debt solution franchise to help people with unmanageable debt problems, where there certainly was market demand. I did well with financially with this business over a two year period and was even offered a board position and shares – not that they ever materialised. The reality was that the 3 day training for new recruits was simply not enough and as the business grew the credibility of the brand was diluted by the poor behaviour of many of the poorly selected and poorly trained consultants. Also the central processing hub did not provide the back office support it had promised and failed to update their archaic manual processes as the business grew.

By which time I had co-founded a business breakfast network, 4Networking.biz for small business owners. Learning from my experiences of how not to do it, and bringing with it my experiences of running my own business and my MBA training I created a scalable business model that allowed the business to grow from a single group to 300 groups across the country, half a dozen in Australia, with an online membership of 50,000 people and a fully paid up membership of 5,000 for the face to face meetings in 5 years from a standing start.

So key questions to ask:-

What are you buying? – Skills training? Mentoring and accountability support? Marketing materials? Access to tools, models and processes? What skill level are the other coaches? What are the pre-requisites to considered entry? If you buy into someone else's model will you be able to live with it, or will you want to "do it your way"?

How will you generate clients? – do you have a thought through lead generation process that goes beyond networking and word of mouth. Do you have a product staircase to make it easy to engage prospects and nurture them into fee generating clients?

What is your business model? Is it based on 1-2-1 coaching of clients face to face on a day rate, a common model but limited by the amount most clients will be willing to pay, or are you able to run a one-to-many program that delivers clear results for a set fee.

What's the business model of the organisation you are considering joining? What's you overall commitment? How could you get out? There is one well know business coaching franchise that requires a large up front franchise fee, and significant marketing fund a high ongoing monthly fee and a tie in for 7 years. Meaning a commitment of over £200,000 over the period. Given that the organisation looks to recruit anyone who has been made redundant with no previous experience, they know many will fail, so they sue the leavers for the contracted sum and re-sell another franchise.

There are the internet marketers who actively promote that you don't need a track record or credibility, that you don't need to share how you'll get a result for your clients, just buy their program and hey presto you can be an internet gazzilionarire too. If that floats your boat, go for it. It's not for me.

Who I am looking for.

I'm at the early stage in widening the reach of my program. I've created it because I couldn't find any programs out there that sensibly combined whole picture business thinking with whole picture personal development. So I created my own. There is simply too much background knowledge to the methodologies and thinking to be able to train a novice. So therefore before even considering being part of the Meaningful Success tribe you will have significant business experience and have done your own work on yourself so that you have heightened self awareness and a deep understanding of self responsibility.

If you are interested in working with me and becoming a meaningful success coach visit www.meaningfulsuccess.co.uk /join

Dr. Jane Cox

Dr. Jane Cox is a world-renowned human behaviours expert, business coach, and a specialist on the psychology of wealth and wealth creation. She is also an in-demand speaker, sharing stages around the world with the likes of Nick Vujicic and Chris Gardner.

A qualified doctor of psychology, with two other doctorates, and several other post-graduate qualifications, she brings a unique blend of theoretical knowledge and real-world expertise. She is the founder of the "Total Life Dynamics" coaching system, and has a cadre of coaches in the UK, Holland, Belgium, South Africa, and the Caribbean.

Jane works with clients on programmes covering wealth, business development, and personal growth, with a focus on creating lasting change; she has a real passion for giving people not just the knowledge they need to make their lives better, but also the methods & tools to make those changes happen. Her passion is helping people to live a life they love.

CHAPTER 9

IT'S ABOUT PEOPLE NOT PROCESS

Dr. Jane Cox

Doing coaching was never part of my plan. I'm a psychologist, for goodness sakes! And I absolutely love psychology. I love finding out how people work, what inspires them, what weighs them down, and what can lift their spirits and inspire them to achieve their greatness.

I was very lucky; for ten years before qualifying as an doctor of Ethnopsychology, I had worked in business, primarily in the fields of public relations, marketing and advertising, and had worked with a wide range of clients, confronting their challenges, understanding their needs, and thinking as laterally as possible to give them the edge in their respective industries, so it was a great opportunity for me to sandwich together my love of business and my understanding of people, and work with businesses as well as with individuals to iron out the wrinkles and help to effectively move them forward. Both of my passions were being filled - working with individuals, and with the cut and thrust of the wonderful world of business!

When I was working with my clients, I figured something else out pretty quickly. When people weren't dealing with things emotionally and mentally, they tended to manifest physical symptoms. I went on to get a doctorate in natural medicine. We are so inextricably linked to our bodies, and they have to last us for our whole lives, so I felt the more I knew and understood, the better.

And then in my quest for completion I decided that if I could now understand people mentally, emotionally and physically, there was just one facet left - spiritually. And so I indulged in my other passion - I studied spiritual philosophy and became a doctor of metaphysics as well. Now I felt I could deal with people from all aspects of themselves, and offer solutions and advice that nurtured all the areas of their lives.

However I found myself coming up with a challenge with every client and with every company that I worked with. What I was doing was unraveling the past, addressing it, freeing up energy and regrets from past mistakes or experiences. I was taking people back through all the burdens that weigh them down, and get then to the point where they can put those burdens down, learn the lessons, understand the experiences, and move on. And it is an exceptionally rewarding thing to do. But now I found that my clients had all their energy back. They were no longer drained and exhausted by holding on to a past that no longer served them. They were eager to move forward into a future that would make them happy, and this got me thinking: How can I help them to move forward as positively as possible, and avoid making the types of mistakes, decisions or actions that may cause them to derail or make decisions that were not going to serve them well in their future?

This is when I started exploring the concept of coaching. What was it actually all about, and where did it fit in with the type of work that I was doing? Pure coaching is all about asking questions, not giving answers. Was there real value in this, and if there was, what was that value? Typically I decided that the only way to properly understand it was to study it, and so I received my first coaching certification from the IHLCA (International Holistic Life Coaching Association).

To be honest, the real benefits of coaching have been taught to me through my experience of working with coaching clients over the last 14 years. For me, coaching perfectly fulfils the role between unburdening people of the past, and consulting people on the future.

What do I mean by that? Well all to often I have seen people putting in huge amounts of work and effort for years and years, only to sit back at the end of the effort and think "what on earth was the point of that!" All of their hard work and sacrifice leaves them feeling empty and unfulfilled, and yet they now feel they have invested too much time, or effort, or reputation, to be able to start over in another field, or change the direction of their lives. And so they feel trapped by their circumstances, stuck on a treadmill that doesn't feel as though it belongs to them.

This is where coaching is so valuable, and this is why I use it so much, not just with clients or businesses who come to me specifically for coaching, but also as a constant method of checking and ensuring that each person and each business is genuinely working towards achieving their dreams. That they are focusing on what brings them happiness and fulfilment, and that they stay true to their chosen path.

We all know how easy it is, especially when the economy is fragile and times are a bit tough, to take on projects, or apply for jobs, or mak personal decisions from a place of desperation, and all of us have probably ended up having to make choices that are not 100% aligned to us at different stages in our lives, but it is so easy for those decisions to not just be one off decisions, but to end up taking you in a completely different direction to what you were planning.

This is definitely where consistent coaching holds huge value. When the coaching client is given the time and space to really think though what they want to do, and assess different options in a safe, confidential and non-judgemental environment, it is a space for them to keep on track, and ensure that they are making decisions and taking actions that are truly valuable and beneficial to them.

However, I couldn't help feeling a bit uncomfortable about two things: Firstly, there were countless "coaches" out there who had hung out their shingle and didn't have any real knowledge or qualifications as a coach. They offered poor value to any clients they attracted, and as happens with so many professions, there is the risk that the under-qualified and lacklustre "coaches" would give the whole profession of coaching a bad name.

Secondly, there were so many coaches out there who seemed to be so bound up in process and procedure, and less concerned about the individual needs and requirements of each client. They followed reams of paperwork, cookie-cutter coaching templates, and methodologies that I'm sure made it easier for them as the coach, but to me were not putting the client as the number one priority in each coaching session.

The whole point of coaching is to ensure that every single client is coached in a way that is person-centric rather than process-centric, and I have always strived to ensure that this is what I do with every single client or business that I coach or consult.

As my coaching practice grew, and my diary filled, I found it challenging, when I was unable to fit a client into my schedule, or if I received an enquiry from a client who was looking for a coach in their area, to find coaches that I knew would treat them with the professionalism that they deserve. I knew that if I referred people to a sub-standard coach, it was my reputation that would be tarnished.

If there is a problem, there must be a solution, and I kept having this nagging feeling that I needed to create the solution that was so important to me. This was when I set up the Total Life Dynamics coaching system, and started training up specially selected individuals who I felt would genuinely make the coaching all about the client. I look for genuine, talented, ethical, professional people who have a drive to help other people make a real success of their lives and their businesses. And I am delighted to have a great team of Total Life Dynamics coaches in a number of different countries, including the Netherlands, Belgium, the United Kingdom and South Africa.

These are ten of the core principles that TLD coaches are taught, and which help them with setting up effective, busy, sustainable coaching businesses in their respective fields of expertise, and I hope that they will benefit you in establishing a successful practice of your own:

> 1. Never lose track of the importance of understanding Life Balance.

Everything in life is a case of give and take, and what can so easily happen is that if a client is hugely focuses on improving one area of their life, other areas may suffer as a result. Always keep an eye on the bigger picture. Huge career progression is great, but not if it leads to relationship damage. Nurtured relationships are fabulous but not if you have lost yourself in the mix. Helping to maintain balance works wonders in creating and maintaining a genuinely happy coaching client.

2. Learn to read the body language behind the words, and what is not said.

Sometimes clients can't articulate what is going on because sometimes they can't figure out why they feel the way they do about a situation they may be facing. Really focus on what your client is telling you through all of their senses, and very importantly: listen to understand, don't just listen to answer!

3. Never assume, always ask.

It sounds obvious, but you'd be surprised how often we become accustomed to assuming that, for example, a person will be feeling a certain way, or wanting a certain outcome, or inspired by something that "most people" find inspiring. But of course each of our clients is unique, and so be aware of what YOU think and be sure to properly explore what THEY think!

4. Each client gets 100%

No matter how tired you are, how many clients you've seen, how often you've said the same thing, and no matter what is going on in your life, that client deserves 100% of your attention. This is their opportunity to put themselves at the centre of their Universe, and you are facilitating that process. It really is ALL about them!

5. If something is outside of your field of expertise or comfort, rather refer that client elsewhere.

I'm fortunate to have three doctorates, and 20-odd years experience working with businesses of my own or others. I am aware this is pretty unusual, but I also know sometimes a challenge I have, is I see my coaches worry that they won't have the knowledge or expertise to answer and have input in all the areas that I can. But of course nobody expects a business coach to understand how to raise teenagers, or a life coach to understand the minutiae of the responsibility of being a director in a firm. You have a whole lot more credibility and enjoy your profession a whole lot more when you do what you do brilliantly, and refer your clients to another expert if and when required. Very often this becomes a reciprocal arrangement between coaches who feel comfortable with each other's levels of professionalism and client service.

6. Be clear with your client if you do consult as well as coach.

Coaching is asking the questions and listening to their answers! So if, like me, coaching is a part of what you do, when you "change hats" and speak as an advisor or consultant, let your client know you are changing your role. It can be done really smoothly and easily - a simple "May I take off my coaches hat and put on my consultant hat?" Allows the client to realise that you are now looking at providing possible answers, which of course is not a part of coaching in it's pure form.

7. Walk your talk! Hold yourself accountable.

All coaches should regularly be coached. This is so important, and I have so often had conversations with other coaches or would-be coaches asking me how to be more successful and create a space for themselves in the coaching industry. You HAVE to do what you would expect your clients to do! Take the actions that grow your business, or improve your personal life, or fix your finances.

8. The client is the one who sets their accountability.

One of the most valuable parts of coaching is the part where, after you have been talking though all the things that are possible, or reviewed the next part of the client's journey, is for them to make a conscious decision on where they are going to use their energy, and where they are going to concentrate on making progress. They will always be more self-motivated if they have committed to their next forward actions, than if you or anyone else is telling them what they should do. At the end of each session, ask your client what they would like to be held accountable for, and then at the beginning of the following session, review that progress.

9. Look the part, behave the part, hold yourself to a high standard.

Have your own set of results in the area/s in which you want to coach!

None of us would want to go for wealth coaching to someone who is battling to pay their rent, or relationship coaching with someone who is permanently unhappy with the state of their relationships. Your life may not be perfect, but probably some parts of it are in a pretty good place, and these areas are probably much more suited to your coaching area of expertise!

10. Your ethics are important.

And while this may sound obvious, there are times when it can be a bit blurry about how we actually work with it. We all have certain beliefs about what is right or wrong. How things should be done or shouldn't be done, and we tend to live our lives according to those premises. However we also know that other people have different sets of belief parameters, and are, on the whole, pretty comfortable with that. The fact is that you have no right to push your set of beliefs onto somebody else, and no right to sit in judgement. You are helping them to live their life in a way that works best for them. So be sure you will not allow your own prejudices stand in the way of a client, but at the same time, if that client stretches your ethics and morals to a point of discomfort, be honest with yourself. You are not doing yourself or your client any favours by working outside of what works for you.

And just to finish this list off, let's look at Confidentiality. Your client needs to be completely open and honest when they are with you. They need to allow themselves to feel vulnerable, expose their weaknesses, own their strengths, and feel completely comfortable, safe and un judged doing so. One of the most important things you can do is completely respect that client confidentiality arrangement. I know that sometimes it can, I feel, be restrictive for me - I could create some great marketing and personal credibility for the work that I do if I could talk about some of the really high-profile companies and individuals who are amongst my clients, but I also know that it would prevent future clients who need that guarantee of silence from seeking out my services. So whether it's a private client working through relationship demons, or a company in the throws of taking over the economic world, confidentially is super important, and by maintaining it, you are showing your respect.

Wherever you are in the world, and whatever area it is you choose to coach, never forget that it is such an amazing privilege to be able to enter the world of so many other people and businesses. To explore and learn about so many different experiences and ideas. So my advice to you, the coach, is to really get stuck into your coaching. Explore it, challenge yourself, and keep learning and growing as an individual.

Every coach I have ever spoken to, and I can literally claim to have spoken to thousands, all agree with one thing: Our experiences with coaching are what make us a great coach. And while it is of course really important to have a solid foundation from which you work, and that formal education that has given you the expertise to start off and hold credibility in this important profession is definitely valuable, it is the learning and growing that coaching gives us that adds real value to our coaching practice.

The coach that you are today, and the coach you will be in five years, are probably very different coaches. Because no matter how good you are today, by holding yourself accountable and continuing to look for ways in which you can continue to facilitate great results from your clients, you will become better, and better.

When you start off with anything, you will not yet be anywhere near the top of your game, but if we "wait until we're perfect", we will never even enter the game. So as with everything else, if you are starting off in coaching, just start! Do your best, keep learning and improving, but start with what you've got and get going. As I am always saying to people, "you will never progress through perfection, you will only perfect through progression!" And so I say the same to you too. Enjoy this incredible profession, and hopefully we will one day be able to meet up and exchange thoughts and experiences of lives well lived!

EFT Master, *Carol Look* is an author, speaker, coach, and creator of her signature coaching method, "The Yes Code." Carol loves helping coaches and lay people release their sabotage behavior so they can move forward in their lives with grace and ease.

Carol is a world-renowned speaker and workshop presenter. She is a frequent guest on Global Telesummits, is featured in the field's leading documentaries on Emotional Freedom Techniques (EFT), and is a primary coach in the movie, Leap. Carol has authored popular books in the EFT field, most notably Attracting Abundance with EFT. She has also created high quality training products to help coaches expand their skills and create lasting results for their clients.

Carol runs her ICF- accredited Yes Code Coach Program for practitioners who are passionate about coaching others to lead lives of exceptional success.

For more on Carol's work, please visit www.CarolLook.com

CHAPTER 10

THE YES CODE

Carol Look, LCSW, Creator of The Yes Code

I wake up every morning to the best job ever – I help other people reach their goals and live their dreams with grace and ease. I have certainly made a million mistakes along the way to reaching my own dreams, and I will undoubtedly make more, but because of my personal experiences and professional training, I have the honor to help coaches, mental health practitioners and lay people live exceptional lives.

I came to the coaching profession as a traditionally trained psychotherapist. I have a Master's Degree in Social work, and have been a psychotherapist for 25 years. After learning how to coach clients using Emotional Freedom Techniques (EFT), and seeing the dramatic shifts in my own life, I became inspired to help people with business and life coaching.

The coaching model I use with my clients is called The Yes Code. I created this coaching method after being frustrated by witnessing people repeatedly sabotage their success, regardless of what kind of coaching they received. The Yes Code Coach Program has been accredited by the International Coach Federation(ICF) and I now teach coaches how to follow the ethical guidelines and core competencies of the ICF. This ensures that their boundaries are impeccable, their skills are of the highest integrity, and they get stellar results.

The Yes Code includes a 5-step process that gives clients the tools and support they need to reach their goals without falling into classic traps such as lack of clarity, setting too many goals, losing focus or trading one sabotage pattern for another.

Step #1 - Choose Your Goal

While this might sound like the most obvious first step of any coaching model, you'd be surprised how many people can't get clear or be specific about their goals. Since we're all complicated with various issues and challenges, and life often feels like a moving target, I understand this challenge. But if this foundation isn't established, the coaching will not "work."

When I start with a new client, I make sure both of us are crystal clear about what specific goal they want to work on during our contracted sessions. If my client has several goals, that's fine, as long as these goals are prioritized and we agree on which goal comes first.

I have found that if this first step hasn't been completed thoroughly, the coaching work is not as effective, and neither coach nor client walks away satisfied. Sometimes it takes more than one session to identify the exact goal(s) the client needs to work on first. Core competencies from the coaching profession such as deep listening, asking powerful questions, and establishing the coaching relationship are key to clarity. Once coach and client agree on the first goal, with a prioritized list of additional goals for later, then I proceed to Step #2 of The Yes Code.

Step #2 - Identify Your Blocks

During this step of The Yes Code, I ask powerful questions to help the client identify what specific blocks are in their way. I also ask what tools have or have not worked before, and assess whether the client is aware that both emotions and behaviors block their success.

Sometimes, this is the step where I learn that a client is a better candidate for psychotherapy than coaching. Coaching is not appropriate for deep childhood trauma, severe depression, anxiety disorders, or complex personality disorders. Whether this information surfaces during Step #1 or Step #2, I refer the client to a psychotherapist who best suits their needs.

Suppose a client contacts a coach and expresses the desire to eliminate procrastination from her life. The client is sick and tired of this behavior, recognizes that procrastination is holding her back, and she feels ready to release this behavioral challenge once and for all.

First I would ask where this behavior block of procrastination shows up – only at work or at home too? Let's follow an example. If the client reveals that she is unable to launch her business website, then I ask my favorite questions:

1. What is the upside of procrastinating?
2. What is the downside of completing this project?
3. How might it be serving you to hold yourself back?

What I know from coaching so many students through The Yes Code Coach Program and examining my own personal behavior is that any self-sabotage behavior – procrastination is a common favorite – is actually solving a problem, or else we wouldn't be doing it. None of our behaviors are frivolous – they are all part of the big picture and add to our conscious or unconscious life plan, which sometimes includes sabotage, failure, and getting in our own way.

Enter coaching... If a client prefers to stay under the radar because she is afraid to fail, afraid to be judged and criticized, or even afraid to shine, then procrastination could "help" her reach this underlying "goal" of staying small.

The point is, once the above questions have been answered, the coach can develop an efficient plan of action with built-in accountability.

Let's go back to the client who seeks coaching to eliminate procrastination. She can't get her website launched, and it has been frustrating her for months.

Here's a sample of how she might answer some of the key questions:

1. What is the upside of procrastinating?
a. I don't have to show up for myself
b. I don't have to find out if I'm a failure

c. I don't have to get feedback
d. I don't have to feel exposed or vulnerable

2. What is the downside to completing your website?
a. I might be more visible
b. I might fail
c. I might stand out and be attacked
d. They'll find out I'm a fraud

3. How does it serve you to continue to procrastinate?
a. I get to play small and protect myself
b. I stay under the radar
c. I don't have to be responsible
d. They won't have any expectations of me

So often I see clients who have never been asked these questions. They have been encouraged to keep pushing through in spite of procrastination. But without identifying what emotions are driving the procrastination, and without the tools to release these underlying fears, the coaching work will not be effective or long lasting. Once we have the information necessary – a clear understanding of the fears that are driving the sabotage behavior – then we can move on to the "clearing" step.

Step #3 - Clear Your Blocks

Now that the client has chosen a specific goal to work on, and identified the blocks that are standing in his or her way, it's time to clear and release these blocks. While there are numerous effective clearing tools out there, I'm going to give you a quick overview and demonstration of a practical clearing tool that changed my life and improved my business dramatically. It's called Emotional Freedom Techniques, or EFT (commonly known as "tapping"). I have been coaching people with EFT for 18 years, and it has allowed me to help others transform their lives quickly, easily, and without all the classic stops and starts that are usually so discouraging.

EFT is a self-help technique that was created in the 1990s by Gary Craig, a personal empowerment coach, and is based on an earlier version of an acupressure technique called Thought Field Therapy, developed by Dr. Roger Callahan (Roger passed away in 2013). The purpose of using the tool is to clear emotional and behavioral conflicts at their core level – in the energy system of the body.

The tool of EFT borrows the theory and methodology of treatment from the ancient Chinese art of acupuncture. Acupuncture treats disruptions in the circuits of energy, or meridians, that transport energy throughout the body, only in EFT, we don't use needles, we use a light tapping motion with our fingertips. While focusing on the issue the client has chosen to release, the coach guides the client to repeat certain phrases and tap on specific acupuncture points on the face and body. This quickly and painlessly releases the energetic conflict stored in the body so that emotional healing can begin and maladaptive behaviors are no longer "needed" by the client.

EFT can be applied to emotional, behavioral, physiological or spiritual issues. The key to this tool's success is being clear and specific, measuring progress methodically, and listening deeply to the client's feedback. Once you have this tool in your toolbox, you can use it for any challenge you have – in or outside of the coaching arena, at home or at work, on yourself or with others – with exceptional results.

Here are the basic steps of EFT:

#1 – Choose your specific target (for example, I'm afraid to fail)
#2 – Measure your distress on the 0-10 point intensity scale
#3 – Devise a setup statement that combines the target with an affirmation. (Even though I have this problem… I deeply and completely love and accept myself...)
#4 - Tap on your karate chop point while repeating the setup statement out loud.
#5 - Tap on face and body points while repeating the reminder phrase (or target)
#6 - Measure your results again, repeat as needed.

Again, this tool has dramatically changed my life and transformed my clients' lives for the better, and they maintain their changes with ease.

Let's run through a classic sample tapping round. Suppose you identify procrastination as a challenge, and releasing it, (which will be measured by you getting your project completed), is your specific definable goal. You've answered the questions and found out that "fear of failure" is the reason you keep procrastinating. You won't launch your website because you think it puts you at risk to be seen as a failure. So in response to "What's the upside of procrastinating?" you answered: "I'm afraid to fail so it seems safer to not complete the project."

First measure how afraid you are of failing – repeat this target statement out loud: "I'm afraid to fail…" and measure it on the 0-10 point scale, (where 10 is totally distressed and 0 is not distressed at all about this topic.) These are the steps to get started with EFT – choose a target and measure the level of distress.

Then put the chosen target into the simple setup statement formula: "Even though I'm afraid to fail, I deeply and completely love and accept myself." Repeat this phrase 3 times while you tap on the karate chop point, (located between the bottom of your pinky finger and the top of your wrist, on either hand).
After repeating the setup statement while tapping on the karate chop point, continue tapping with your fingertips on the sequence of acupuncture points listed below while repeating a version or variations of the target statement, in this case, "I'm afraid to fail."

Eyebrow Point (at the beginning of either eyebrow) – I'm afraid to fail
Side of Eye (outside of either eye) – I'm afraid I'm going to fail
Under Eye (on bony orbit under eye) – I'm afraid to fail
Under Nose (on your upper lip) – I don't want to finish my website
Chin Point (between chin and lower lip) – I'm afraid to fail, so why bother
Collarbone Point (one inch below bumps at end of collarbone) –No wonder I procrastinate
Under Arm (4 inches below your armpit) – I'm afraid to fail
Top of Head (on the top of your head) I'm afraid to fail

Repeat the target statement out loud again, I'm afraid to fail, and measure your results on the 0-10 point scale. If your fear of failure was initially an 8, where does it land on the scale now as you tune in again? For most people, if they've followed the directions and stayed focus, it will have decreased in intensity.

Repeat the above steps, shifting your target statement if necessary, and continue with the tapping sequences until you no longer feel afraid to

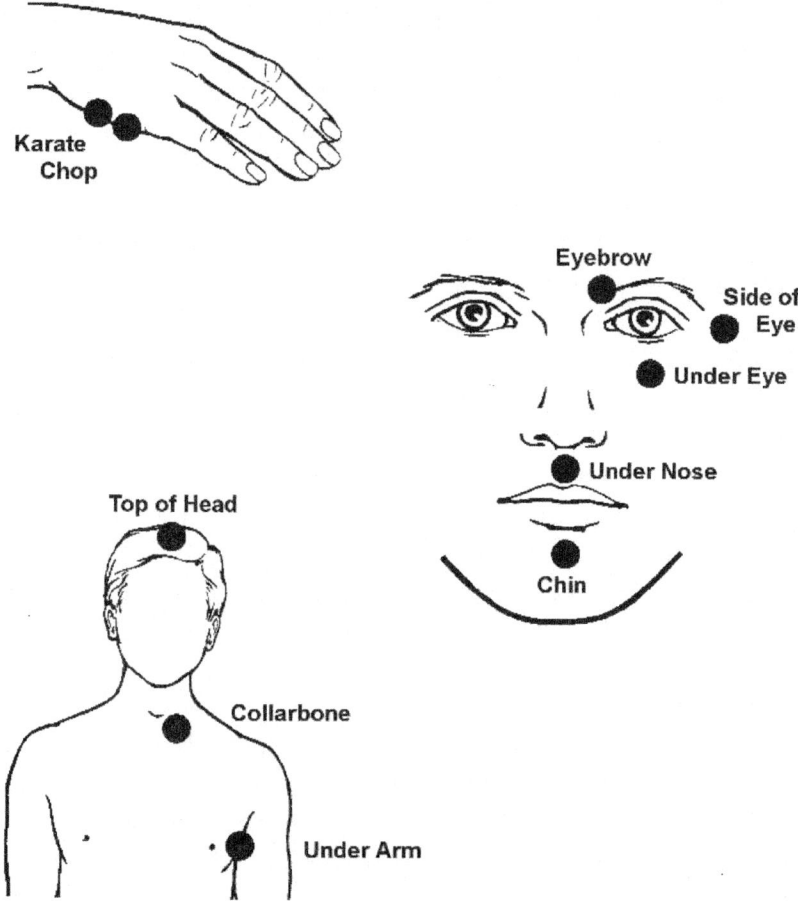

fail and the thought of completing your website (or any other project) feels inspiring rather than intimidating.

You may apply this simple, practical coaching tool to any of your emotional blocks or sabotage behaviors that keep you from reaching your goals.

Now let's move on to the next step of The Yes Code.

Step #4 - Find Your Next Yes

Being able to recognize and find your next yes is another key step on the journey to reaching your goals. Suppose your client's fear of failure (or yours) was so "loud" that she never realized she was pursuing the wrong niche in business. Perhaps she was marketing to new mothers who wanted to get back into the workforce, but her passion is really serving female entrepreneurs. But behind all the noise of the fear, she never heard this "yes." Now that the primary block, fear of failure, has been cleared, she can start the process of examining goals, choosing the right action steps, and recognizing what a real "yes" in her gut feels like.

Unfortunately, many of us have had decades of practice ignoring or denying the "yes" answer from within. If you don't know what a "yes" feels like inside of you, try this exercise.

Close your eyes, and think of your favorite person in the world. Now feel how your body and inner world feel… Calm? Quiet? Peaceful? Happy? This feeling can now become your measurement of what a "yes" feels like to you. A "yes" never feels agitated, disturbed or conflicted.

Now picture someone you are challenged by or don't trust, and go inside your mind and body again, and see how that feels to you. Agitated? Disturbed? Stressful? That feeling can now be your baseline measurement of a "no" which you will be able to recognize after this exercise. I highly recommend practicing this skill with small decisions in your life – if you can't find your next yes on a daily basis, you certainly won't be able to live the life of your dreams.

Practice this again with your favorite and least favorite colors, or with a project you are looking forward to and one you dread. This is how you will start to measure and recognize your inner "yes and no" so you can make the right decisions to move forward in your life.

Before you take any next step towards your goal, wait until you get a clear "yes" or "no" inside of you for each small step. The process will flow much more easily, and you might actually have fun along the way!

Step #5 - Voice Your Gratitude

While you are moving towards your goal, I highly recommend that you Voice Your Gratitude – to yourself, out loud, or on paper – to access this incredible energetic frequency. Gratitude is truly a game-changer as far as loving life and managing the ups and downs that our friends, family, and job send our way. Accessing the power of gratitude is an integral part of The Yes Code Coach Program.

In business, I recommend that clients make a gratitude list about their product launches before they start the launch – if you don't have 10 positive things to say about your own book or seminar, then other people won't either.

I recommend that parents make a gratitude list about their moody teenager. If your adolescent is constantly feeling your annoyance and dismissiveness, good luck trying to set boundaries with them.

And instead of trying to punish yourself into losing weight, make a gratitude list about your body – how strong and stable it is, how much you appreciate it – before starting to deny it foods and force it to go to the gym for you!

My favorite gratitude techniques are as follows:

1. The Gratitude List
Buy a colorful journal for your expressions of gratitude, and make the commitment to write every day. You can vary this list from "10 things I feel grateful about" to "10 things I love about my life." The words aren't as important as the sentiment and follow through. In time, I promise you will feel inspired to write your gratitude list, and you won't want to miss it!

2. The Gratitude Walk
This is a variation on the gratitude list. Instead of writing down what you appreciate, voice your gratitude list out loud while you're walking outside. Take a nice stroll and notice the trees, flowers, dogs and children and voice your gratitude out loud. (If you're worried about other people's reactions, trust me, they won't be bothered if they hear you talking to yourself.)

3. The Gratitude Grid
I originally learned the grid work directions from the Abraham-Hicks teachings. Take a piece of paper and draw a huge box on it. Then draw 3 evenly spaced horizontal lines and 3 evenly spaced vertical lines inside. This will leave you with 16 separate boxes. In each box, write a feeling or state of mind you want to experience today. In the upper left hand corner, you could write "freedom" and below that "appreciation" and in the next box, "ease." Fill in all the boxes in any order with any feelings or words you want. I often put "magic" or "miracles" in my boxes, along with "relief" "peace" and "joy."

While all these gratitude recommendations are incredibly easy to do, many people don't actually do them consistently. If you want your life to become more peaceful, your relationships to improve and your goals to seem more manageable, use one of these simple exercises to access the frequency of gratitude in your life. Again, it is truly a game-changer.

So this concludes the 5 steps of my signature coaching method, The Yes Code, that has changed thousands of lives quickly, efficiently, and consistently.

Enjoy!
Carol Look, Author, Speaker, Coach, Creator of The Yes Code

Kristin Grayce McGary is an author, speaker, trainer, and expert in holistic, comprehensive, functional, and individualized health care. She speaks on diverse topics, including functional blood chemistry analysis, ketogenic gut repair, and The 10 Shocking Reasons You May be Sick and Tired so that you can become an informed and empowered advocate for your and your family's health care. She weaves over 20 years of experience, education, wisdom, and profound compassion to provide opportunities to heal on all levels. She artfully blends dozens of healing modalities such as acupuncture, homeopathy, advanced craniosacral and somatoemotional release therapies, Lifeline technique, dolphin assisted therapy, and extensive lifestyle and nutritional support, to guide you on a transformative path to optimal wellness. She embodies her work through authentic relating practices, five-element sacred cacao meditations, Argentine tango, Tribal style belly dance, and cycling. She is a wife, mother, and grandmother.
www.kristinmcgary.com

CHAPTER 11

TIPS FOR AUTHENTIC COACHING SUCCESS

Kristin Grayce McGary

One of the first questions I ask coaches, holistic healthcare practitioners and my patients is "Why do you do what you do?". Knowing your "why" in coaching and holistic healthcare forms a strong foundation for attracting your perfect clients and thereby creating a larger impact on the world. Understanding the reasons why you act as you do in any area of your life—and in any relationship—profoundly impacts how events unfold, which can make or break your business development and your vibrant health. They care less about your story and how you achieved health or wealth, than they doa bout their own story, and how they will get relieve and results. I don't want to hold anything back from you so I'm going to dive right in with a few tips. First, explore every "why" you have, the generous, altruistic, compassionate ones, and the selfish, ego-driven ones. Every "why" is important. A few questions to consider: Do you have a passion for helping people? Do you feel better about yourself when you help others? How do you personally benefit from offering your gifts? Do you want income? Credentials? Accolades? Community respect? Knowing about these parts of yourself creates influential vulnerability that attracts just the right people to you. Influential vulnerability is a kind of vulnerability that greatly influences your connection and impact on others. You might find opportunities to share these personal motives with your clients, or you might not, but you should still know your own mind and heart. As befits your personal and business style, it might be important to share these personal (and perhaps vulnerable) truths while continuing to position yourself as an expert with the experience, skill, strength, hope, and wisdom to profoundly benefit your clients.
Ever since the tender age of two, I knew I wanted to alleviate suffering

and help people heal. I have a photograph of myself as a toddler using a stethoscope on my grandmother's forearm, at the very place where Tibetan doctors take pulses. My goal was always to attend medical school and become a doctor. After working in the Emergency room as an Emergency Medical Technician (EMT), and later becoming debilitated with a severe chronic illness, I saw beyond the Western medical model. My personal health journey—where I regained health, balance, and vitality in body, mind, and spirit—strongly informs what I share and how I practice. As I walked alternative paths that helped me, I wanted to share what I learned.

Western medicine is incredible and is especially suited to saving the lives of those suffering acute injury and trauma. However, I was disheartened to learn that it fared poorly with chronic and degenerative conditions, and often inflicted harm—especially through drug treatments—even as it saved lives. I learned this through my studies of homotoxicology and biological medicine from experts like Dr. Thomas Rau and Dr. Dietrich Klinghardt. I recognized both the benefits and the hazards of the Western medical model and I wanted something more comprehensive and integrated. I intuitively understood that exercise and nutrition played a part, but I didn't yet fully understand how. I am an athlete. In my late teens and early twenties, I was a competitive body builder and vegetarian. I played soccer and softball, I swam, ran, cycled, and lifted weights, and yet I was getting sicker. I didn't understand how this could happen to someone who led such a healthy lifestyle. I was diagnosed with fibromyalgia by a rheumatologist in Washington, DC during my junior year of college. I finally had a diagnosis, reassuring me that it wasn't all in head. Now, I began the arduous journey to discover the root cause of my debilitating symptoms, heal, and peel that "sick" label off my forehead. I had been suffering with acute and chronic trigger-point pain all over my body. I would randomly go into spasms and for days be unable to function--even to brush my own hair. I had painful temporal mandibular joint (TMJ) dysfunction. I wasn't sleeping well. I had migraines. I had severe fatigue. I had chronic stomach aches, gas and bloating. I gained 30 pounds, mostly as a side-effect of pain medications. I had brain fog and lost my words during conversations. My relationships suffered, and my dream to attend medical school was fading. I began searching for alternatives to the Western drugs for pain. I found chiropractic, which led me to acupuncture and craniosacral therapy, Qigong, martial arts, somato-emotional release, homeopathy, biological medicine, herbs, trauma work, functional blood chemistry analysis, shamanism, non-violent communication. Later, I found hydrogen peroxide therapy, chelation therapy, holotropic breathwork, LifeLine technique, apitherapy, dolphin-assisted therapy. I explored spiritual practices through Pema Chodron, "The Work" by Byron Katie, Ken Wilber's Integral model, authentic relating practices, and many more. I discovered that the symptoms of fibromyalgia were actually associated with heavy metal toxicity, Epstein Barr virus, autoimmune Hashimoto's thyroiditis, and many subconscious patterns that blocked my body's ability to heal. And so I did the work to dive deeply into myself, my relationships and my career, while doing my best to raise my newborn son as a single mother. Over time, I accomplished what the Western medical doctors told me was impossible: I healed. This is my "why". I felt so passionate about the miracles that had occurred in my body—against all odds, contradicting what the doctors had told me—that I knew this was what I must share with the world. I was bursting with desire to make a difference in people's lives. I wanted them to experience the kind of transformation that I had invited, struggled with, and eventually surrendered to. It was from this place of deep conviction, that I entered Oriental medical school, then trained in advanced craniosacral and somato emotional release, biological medicine, homeopathy, and functional healthcare. At first I offered what had directly benefited me and then expanded my education to include many more healing tools. I began to embody and model these healing approaches and share them with others, offering hope, empowerment, and compassion through scientifically informed, holistic, comprehensive, individualized, and patient-centered care. I feel fulfilled, honored, and excited to support you in your unique journey to discover, refine, and offer your gifts to the world, walking a deeply rewarding path while making powerful impact in the world.

Education and training are essential. Competence in your field is the foundation for attracting clients. And I learned a long time ago that you only need to be one or two steps ahead of your ideal clients to help them get amazing results and refer others to you. I graduated from the Arizona School of Acupuncture and Oriental Medicine with a Diplomat in Acupuncture and Oriental Medicine and later, a Master's degree in Acupuncture. I'm nationally board certified and licensed in the states of Arizona and Colorado. I currently sit on the Colorado State Acupuncture

Association Board. I studied and practiced advanced craniosacral and somato-emotional release therapies, biological medicine, electro-dermal screening techniques, shamanism, and much more. I am an Enneagram 7, and therefore have a great desire and capacity to study and integrate information. I learn healing modalities quickly and in great depth. I know that some coaches and healthcare providers think they need more certifications in order to put themselves out into the coaching or healthcare world. I thought I had to take class after class to somehow prove to myself and my patients that I was trained and was finally good enough to help them. What I have come to appreciate is that my inner journey around competency was just as powerful as the professional health and medical classes I paid to attend. Certainly, those courses helped me build a tool box full of modalities that have helped many hundreds of people heal and transform their lives. And I've learned that my being present, compassionate, loving, authentic, and grounded are also therapeutic and highly valuable skills.

Success has numerous dimensions beyond money and prestige, especially personal growth, community empowerment, and direct healing impact on clients. Inner work and personal growth to harmonize emotional blocks, fixations, triggers, and shadow-self sabotage bring personal satisfaction and amplify your capacities for coaching, business deals, and healing work. A successful outcome in this sphere can be as simple as taking a risk to speak up publicly about a topic of common concern, or giving voice to a vulnerable emotion that you would otherwise hold inside or suppress, or enhancing your self-care, or training in a healing modality, or learning how to effectively promote and run a business. Beyond the traditional measures of money and prestige, outer success can be achieved by impact. The many ways you positively affect your family, staff, professional colleagues, community, and world make beautiful success stories.

My patients and I fulfill our personal-growth needs through many practices such as authentic relating, tracking our awareness, and thereby receiving profound gifts of insight, transformation, and healing. I will now offer three valuable tips to completely shift the way you attract ideal clients, how you work with them, and the results you achieve. The foundation is honest awareness of self, other, and environment, which builds connection and trust.

Tip #1: Know if your client is a good fit for you.

It's common to fear scarcity, which can lead you to take on even when it's not the right fit. I have learned it is important to interview potential patients to determine if I am the right healthcare provider for them. You must learn the client's "what" and "why"—what does your potential client desire, why do they want that, and are they ready to work to achieve it. I ask questions during my Free Optimal Wellness Consultation that helps me identify the stuck spots. (I learned some of these questions from Thrive Academy and my dear mentors Jesse Koren and Sharla Jacobs.) I ask a potential client this:

What are the greatest issues you wish to address? Pay close attention to concerns regarding money, health, and relationships.

What have you done to resolve these issues, and how did it work out?

How are these issues impacting your life, especially in health, business, and relationships?

What is the financial, emotional, physical, and mental costs of not resolving these issues?

I invite the client to use their imagination, like an innocent child playing with friends, and imagine their life in the most ideal and fulfilling way. What picture do they paint?

I ask them to connect to the emotion that arises when they connect to that imagined life. It's feeling as if it has already happened. The emotions should be positive, but if not, they should reconnect with their dream-come-true.

I ask how committed are you, on a scale of 0-10, to achieving your ideal. Conducting this inquiry should give both you and your potential client a good feel for what they need and how well you might work together. If you encounter too much resistance to identifying their issues, or insufficient commitment to healing them, I find it best that they work with someone else.

Tip #2: Identify and dissolve any and all concerns.

Over the past twenty years, I have come to deeply appreciate the process of identifying concerns and addressing them. The most common concerns pertain to money, time, self-image, the opinions of others, fear of failure, and even fear of success. Many offer the concern that they don't have enough money to work with you. While possibly valid, in my experience there is usually something else beneath the surface, and money surfaces only to mask for the true concerns. I am not suggesting that you needle a reluctant client, but rather you hold the sacred space to help them reach a crystal clear choice, free of fear. Do not stop at "maybe", and continue seeking clarity. Vulnerability and full disclosure is key. Invite them to dive into their "maybe" and find what they need in order to make a decision. Asking someone to choose is bold and empowering, and they will respect you more for guiding them to clarity. This is not a sales pitch—you must put your own agendas aside and be a clear neutral channel for their own process of discovery. If you have personal agendas, they will sense that and instinctively pull back. If you can authentically detach from the outcome, and focus completely on them, the process will be so powerful that even if they choose not to work with you, they will likely refer their closest friends and business partners to you. You must dissolve any concerns that arise in conversation, and you can dissolve them even before that, when you sense their concerns are first coming to mind. When a concern arises (money, for example) invite them to imagine that their concern didn't exist and if they would then choose to work with you. This will help you find if there are more concerns beneath the surface. I always begin with empathy for their fear around the concern, then find ways to inspire confidence and hope for plausible solutions, often giving examples from my personal experience or from the experience of a past client (preserving that client's privacy, of course!). A common hidden concern in my field is that they are afraid it will be too difficult to change too many things in their diet. I breathe a sigh of relief when I hear this one because I have so much experience with diet and nutrition, I know I can solve nearly any problem. For example, I might say, "I know that many people are afraid of making huge changes to their diet, it can feel scary and overwhelming. I know that for me it was as simple as removing celery, walnuts and bananas and my body responded positively and quickly."

Tip #3: Connect to your deepest desire, discover what brings you pleasure and ask for what you want.
In the previous tip, I advised you to put your agendas aside in order to serve your potential client to discover their deep desires and concerns. In the context of a consultation, this is professional, ethical, and effective. However, outside that specific client-focused context, it is imperative that you attend to your desires and needs, to find pleasure in your work and your life. Deep desire and transcendent pleasure need to be

at the heart of your internal guidance system. The desires I speak of are those that nurture and empower you, not addictive ones that drain and distract you. For example, I feel pleasure when I work out, because it helps me feel strong, healthy, and grounded in my body. I love sitting in nature, because it brings me peace, calm, and connection to all of creation. I enjoy working with clients when there is a good fit, because we exchange value, and mutually celebrate healing and empowerment. All of these experiences are deeply rooted in my whole being. They are pleasurable in all dimensions of body, mind, heart, and spirit, and every chakra from root to crown is engaged. When I really get in touch with this deep and multi-faceted sense of pleasure and use it to inform and guide my actions, amazing things unfold for me and my clients. This is much more than a quick fix, superficial pleasure; like that of an addict getting high and feeling pleasure. Failure to connect with this whole-being pleasure in business, relationships, health, and personal growth leaves us vulnerable to disconnection and burn-out. I often use bodily sensations and somato-emotional experiences as my guidance system. Whereas my mind can trick me and override my best interests, my body does not deceive me. Tension, contraction, heaviness, and pain offers vital information about my thinking and actions, so I pay attention. If I am working with someone and always feel horrible after each interaction, then it's time to take a deeper look at what may be going on. It may be that they are triggering a deep wound or a shadow aspect of my being. Or it may be that I am somehow out of integrity with myself. Finally, identifying what I truly desire greatly increases my chances of getting it. Sometimes what I truly desire is within my own power to provide for myself, and sometimes I must ask others. I never expect others to produce what I want, but because I'm carefully listening to my authentic internal pleasure guidance system, I am often happily surprised that people respond so openly to my requests. What I find is that many people are inherently generous, just as you and I are, and enjoy giving, just as you and I do. When we ask for something, remember that we are creating an opportunity for someone to follow their deep desire to give and to serve the world with love. Now that's a win/win!

In my experience, the key to success as a coach or health care practitioner is deep knowledge in multiple dimensions. You must know of your own needs and desires. You must discover your clients' hopes and fears, and dance with both. You must dive into a wide variety of business models, coaching styles, and healing modalities that collectively address all aspects of business, body, mind, and spirit, enabling you to cover all the bases when weaving an individualized business or healing treatment plan. The other experts in this book are a valuable resource to rounding out your own business-coaching approach. Knowledge is power. You can use that power to effect lasting transformation to greatly benefit your own life and the lives others.

Thomas Gelmi

Thomas Gelmi stands for measurably more impact in leadership, teamwork and customer interaction by developing personal and interpersonal competence. With almost three decades of professional experience and a track record of more than fifteen years in the field of learning and development, Thomas has trained and coached leaders on all levels, mainly in Europe but also in the U.S., Canada, the Middle East, Asia, Australia and Africa. Based in Switzerland, his full proficiency in four languages (En, Ge, It, Fr) combined with excellent international references makes him a highly sought after, reliable partner for individuals and organizations across various industries and cultures. Client partnerships include global corporations like Siemens, Roche, Syngenta, Ford, Swiss Re and Credit Suisse, numerous SMEs and private clients.

Contact information:
Thomas Gelmi - InterPersonal Competence
Movadis GmbH, Europaallee 41, 8021 Zurich, Switzerland
Tel: +41 56 535 7996, Web: www.thomasgelmi.com

CHAPTER 12

BE THAT 'SOMEONE'...
"WHAT WE REALLY NEED IS SOMEONE WHO CAN BRING OUT THE BEST IN US."

Thomas Gelmi

This interpretation of a quote by Ralph Waldo Emerson perfectly describes the essence of my approach in coaching. With almost three decades of professional experience and more than fifteen years in the field of learning and development, I am so honored to have journeyed with and supported numerous executives, managers and leaders on various levels, across continents, from diverse cultures and in varied industries.

Two areas of development
In my vocation, I focus on two main areas of development: personal and interpersonal competence. The ability to truly connect with others and to build and maintain relationships is a key success factor in leadership, teamwork and customer interaction. I am convinced that the necessary interpersonal competence can only be developed on the basis of solid personal or self-competence, which includes self-awareness, self-knowledge and self-management. As a professional coach, my mission is to facilitate growth in these two areas.

As with many coaches, I employ a range of formats such as one-on-one sessions with individuals, group sessions with management teams and workshops or training events with groups of participants. In all of these settings, I adopt a coaching attitude where I see myself as a professional sparring partner who acts as a sounding board, asks the questions, provides inspiration and gives constructive input. In understanding, coaching can be viewed as a form of acupuncture: with small interventions in the right spots, blockages are released and insights gained allowing clients to become unstuck and get back 'in the flow' or step into the next level of their development.

On a personal note
My official career as a coach started about 15 years ago, while in retrospect I started coaching much earlier. In my late teenage years, I earned my first income as a hairstylist. During my three years of professional training, I was privy to many personal and intimate stories of my clients – and sometimes more than I actually wanted to know. So, what I basically did was a lot of listening, which is of course a key element in coaching. It was only much later that I understood how these were actually my first 'coaching interventions'. I remember people telling me how good it felt and how helpful it was to be talking to me. Ironically, at the time, I felt quite lost when it came to my own calling and professional career. I never really knew what was "the right thing to do" for me.

The years that followed were an odyssey of trial and error of job experiences. I worked for a circus and lived in a trailer, built and managed a tele-sales department with 40 sales agents and worked for an employment agency. None of these jobs felt like a good fit. Then, one day, I saw a job ad by Swissair, the former Swiss national airline. They were seeking flight attendants and immediately I knew that this was going to 'fly' for me. Being fluent in four languages, I applied and got the job. Over the next seven years I flew around the world, first as a flight attendant and later as a "Maître de Cabine" with responsibility for crew leadership, service quality and passenger safety. During these exciting years I learned a great deal about myself, about people and cultures, about leadership, teamwork and customer interaction, about what works in human interaction and what does not. As you can appreciate, personal and interpersonal competence is crucial in a metal tube with 300 people at 35,000 ft. above sea level. Problems need to be anticipated and solved on the spot, without external assistance, and by maintaining the relationships.

Subsequent to the grounding of Swissair in 2001, I left the company and started working for a small consultancy in Zurich with a focus on leadership development in sales. I focused on my own development and further education, attained a diploma in General Management, a Swiss Federal Diploma as a Leadership Expert and earned a number of well-recognized HR development certifications in training, coaching and diagnostics such as Marshall Goldsmith's Stakeholder Centered Coaching and Global Leader of the Future (GLOF) Assessment, Hogan Assessments, the PCM Process Communication Model, Solution-focused Brief Coaching, Provocative Coaching, etc. I am a certified member of the International Coach Federation (ICF) and regularly write blogs and articles for various specialist journals.

Currently, I work with large multi-national corporations covering a wide range of industries. My list of clients includes Siemens, Roche, Syngenta, Ford, Credit Suisse, Swiss International Airlines, Swiss Re, Expedia, and Red Bull amongst others. I also support private individuals in their career development and coaches in developing and growing their businesses.

Coach to Coach
Here are my personal recommendations for you, if you want to start growing your own business as a coach.

Start with what you have
Two of the most hindering beliefs that are likely to keep you from being successful as a coach are:
I am not quite there yet.
I have it.

Let us address each of these beliefs. I have personally encountered many coaches who believe that they are not quite ready to start coaching. Mostly because they think they do not have the necessary skills, qualifications or certifications yet and because they are not yet accredited by one of the major coaching bodies. This perspective may stem from seeking to operate from an ethical basis being legally qualified, working to the correct standards, and where logic determines that it is more acceptable to first learn something before you go out into the world to apply it. Let me make a distinction here between qualification and competence. Qualification is what you get when you attend coaching training and become certified. You learn about basic attitudes in coaching, about tools, methods and techniques. Competence is what you develop by applying all of this, by actually coaching other people. Studies have shown that up to 70% of what we are capable of is not acquired at school or through further education and training, but on-the-job, by getting up in the morning and going out into the world to face challenges and solve problems (Bernd Overwien, 2005). This is especially true in coaching. You need the actual experience to learn. And in coaching there are always at least two parties who learn: the coachee and the coach. The more you coach, the better you get at coaching.

Especially in the beginning, this may require you to step out of your comfort zone, particularly if you believe that you are "not quite there yet". You may feel a little uncomfortable offering your support to others while at the same time carrying this hindering belief within you. This is not necessarily a bad thing, because if you think of personal development and growth, where does this happen? Inside or outside the comfort zone? You already know the answer.... So, in other words, being outside the comfort zone is the best place to learn. And therefore, becoming comfortable with being uncomfortable is what you should be aiming for.

Naturally, you should seek to learn methods and techniques and to attain your coaching training qualifications. But at the same time you should gather as much experience as you can because tools and techniques are just one element of great coaching. Other aspects are presence, self-awareness, curiosity and a beginner's mind or state of "not knowing". This last aspect can be especially helpful in taking those first steps outside of the comfort zone. As a coach, you are not supposed to know all the answers to your client's questions. You are supposed to be the one asking the questions; significant questions, useful questions. And not knowing is a good place to start when it comes to asking questions.

Which brings me directly to the second hindering belief that keeps coaches from being successful: "I have it". This is the belief that you have learned enough, know enough and have enough experience so that you do not have to take any further steps in your own development. One of the key messages, in a great book by Marshall Goldsmith entitled "What Got You Here Won't Get You There", is that we often tend to believe that we are successful because of what we do and how we behave (i.e., what got us here), while at the same time ignoring that we are also successful despite certain actions and behaviors. If we are not open to these blind spots and do not examine them closely, they are likely to keep us from being even more successful (i.e., getting there). In order to do this, you need to maintain a sense of humility, especially when you have already grown to be successful. Continuous feedback and feedforward provided by a supervisor or mentor can be one helpful aspect in reducing your own blind spots and keeping you in the beginner's mindset.

In a nutshell: start coaching. Start from where you are and with what you have. You are ready at any given moment. Keep a beginner's mindset while you grow, stay humble and curious and avoid settling down inside the comfort zone.

Change your view on selling
Many coaches I meet are great coaches; however, selling their services leaves room for improvement. This often relates to how they view sales. If you think of sales as a pushy and aggressive way of manipulating others towards emptying their pockets in order to get what you want, then evidently selling is not the most attractive attribute of your coaching business. As with most things, sales can be regarded from different perspectives. And given that you as a coach help your clients to change perspective - well, it is certainly worth the effort for you to challenge your personal view on sales.

When it comes to promoting your coaching business it is important to bear in mind that this is a people's business. Coaching is about engaging in helpful and useful conversations, about creating a safe environment or space in which, often, very personal and intimate topics can be openly shared and discussed. This is not a commodity. It requires openness and vulnerability and at the end of the day it all comes down to relationships and trust.

So, how do we build trust? Usually we build trust over time and by repeatedly experiencing behaviors that confirm trustworthiness. Distributing marketing flyers or making cold calls is indisputably not very effective. Instead, a personal experience is required. People need to experience you as a person. They need to experience how they feel in your presence and whether they could imagine opening up to you and sharing their concerns.

The following three distinguishing phases will assist you in promoting your coaching services:

1. Do not make it about you – MAKE IT ABOUT THEM
Let's say I am a potential client and I am looking for a coach. Probably the first thing I would do is ask my network who they know. In addition, I might ask my friend Google, who will offer hundreds if not thousands of search results. Most likely I will have a closer look at the first few results. My experience at this juncture is key. Subconsciously I will ask myself: can I identify with the person I see on this website and does the website content talk about me and my needs? This is where many coaches already fail. The information on many coaching websites revolves mainly around the coach, the business or the offering rather than targeting their potential clients' needs and how they can solve them. Make your online presence about your clients. Let them see that you identify with their pain points and that you understand their needs. This will create trust and the willingness to meet you in person. Your online presence does not necessarily sell your services. Instead, it opens the door to a first personal experience.

2. Don't sell coaching – COACH
So, I got a good impression from your online presence, I visited your website, saw your LinkedIn profile and read a bit about you in your blog. And I invited you to have a conversation. This is where you can show who you are and how you work. Not by selling coaching, but by doing what you do. Avoid applying any sales techniques to "close the deal" and to come across as pushy. Especially for potential clients higher up in the hierarchy this may cause irritation and resistance. Remember, this is about relationship and trust. Don't sell coaching - COACH. Enquire about the other person's goals and expectations for the conversation and guide the conversation as if it already was your first coaching session. Allow them to experience what it will feel like to be coached by you – and make them want more of that.

3. Hope is not a strategy – ASK for what you need
Today, 9 out of 10 coaching clients come to me by recommendation. This is by far the most effective way of getting new clients. Why? Simply because the first hurdle of building trust was already taken – by someone else. Has a good friend of yours ever recommended a restaurant to you?

It is highly unlikely that you would first check the respective internet portals to see whether your friend's recommendation is justifiable, right? Instead you probably trust your friend's recommendation and expect that the great experience he or she had will likely be the same for you. Undoubtedly, for this to happen in your service offering, you need to do a good job first. This is what most coaches are good at. Now let's assume you did a great job and your client is pleased and satisfied. What do you do next? I am guessing that you hope that your client will at some point recommend you to someone else? Well, this may happen eventually. But hope is not a strategy. It is very likely that after shaking hands and saying thank you, your client will go back to focusing on other things. The question "who could I recommend XY to?" is not very likely to be on top of your client's mind. Unless – you ask for it.

I often ask my clients at the end of a coaching process, and depending on the client sometimes even during a coaching assignment: "Who do you know that could have an interest in talking to me?" Or: "What are the first two names that come to your mind that could have an interest in talking to me?" or "Who would you be willing to introduce me to?" Usually, people are willing to help when they are asked such a specific question. They may say that they will have to think about it. However, very often I get at least one or two contacts. I can then either approach them referring to my existing client, or my client will actively introduce me to them. This is by far the most powerful and effective way of promoting your coaching services.

Last but not least: Increase your visibility
Let's take inventory. You are an awesome coach. You have chosen to discard your hindering beliefs and have started with what you got. What good is this if nobody knows that you exist? If you do not increase your visibility and constantly keep it high, people will not know that you are always there for them as an option or they may forget about you.

Systematically using social media is one of the ways in which you can maintain visibility. In the same way as your website, your social media profiles and activities are not necessarily the means or tools to actively sell your services. Ever confirmed a connection request on LinkedIn, only to be sent an aggressive sales pitch three minutes later? Not pleasant, right? Once again, this is not about actively selling and being pushy but about creating awareness of who you are and what you offer, in order to generate interest and create a pull effect. The goal is to remain present on your potential clients' minds, so they think of you first whenever they develop a need.

Personal engagement is a highly effective way to maintain visibility. Here is an example of how this works for me: besides my work as a coach, I also teach at various Swiss business schools. The good thing about this teaching activity is that the attendees of these learning programs have a first experience with me. They get to know me personally and they experience my working style. At some point, the learning experience is over and they return to their jobs and organizations. Because we are connected through social media, they regularly see me 'popping up' with either my own content or third-party content which is relevant to what I do. At some point, a need may arise. Something like "We should definitely start developing our leadership skills more systematically – who knows of a coach we could ask for a concept?" This is the moment where high visibility pays off. The awareness as a possible provider is either immediate, or at the next visible social media post, and the contact is established.

If you put all of this into practice, take it step-by-step and believe in yourself, it will only be a matter of time before you will be running a successful coaching business.

Now, go out there and be that 'someone' who brings out the best in others!

Michael A. Pomije, PCC

Michael A. Pomije, PCC is a Professional Certified Coach (PCC) credential by (ICF) and is an Executive Life Coach, Facilitator and Mentor.

He believes that through coaching and training, people can learn how to transform themselves into powerful individuals, discovering their passion, and maintaining balance in their personal and professional lives.

Married since 1993, one of his favorite coaching topics is creating successful and satisfying relationships. Michael brings his experiences to his coaching practice to support executives in optimum health, achieving results, managing family demands, and work-life balance. With his love of traveling, he trains in US, Asia, and Europe with the ACTP and ASCTH programs (accredited by ICF). He holds a BA degree in Business Management. He would never ask of his clients to push their limits he didn't lead the way.

CHAPTER 13

MASTERING CROSS-CULTURAL COACHING ABROAD EXECUTIVE & LIFE COACHING ON THE ROAD!

Michael A. Pomije, PCC

When I was 10 years old, my mother and her friends invited me to accompany them to the high school stadium in our neighborhood to "walk the track" and do light calisthenics. I was mildly shocked that I was the only child included in this "ladies" group. I was sworn to secrecy because in those days women didn't exercise since it was not considered ladylike.

I liked hanging out with mom and the other women. I was interested in listening to their stories about their families and their weight loss. I also liked feeling my strength, capability, perceived invincibility at such a young age.

Both experiences planted seeds in me for the rest of my life.

If you don't have your health you don't have anything! It doesn't matter how much money you have, nor does it matter how powerful you become. It doesn't matter if your name is an international brand or if your fan club in social media is over a million. If you don't have your health you're missing the most important thing in life!

When I met Dr. Chérie Carter-Scott I shared with her that I wanted to take a personal development workshop so that I could truly be in alignment with myself, my values, my principles, and my direction in life. I signed up for her Inner Negotiation Workshop, known to many as the "INW" in which I could release some of my issues regarding not living up to my expectations of myself. Taking the Inner Negotiation Workshop allowed me to "Reset" my life from the inside out, to truly respect myself, to find my self-confidence, and to align with my overall vision and goals. I reclaimed what was rightfully mine!

Enthusiastically, two months later, I signed up for my first official 12-week coach training course in 1990 in California with the MMS Institute. That was in the early days, before coaching was considered a profession. ICF wasn't even conceived until five years later.

Throughout my life people have always come to me and asked, "How do you stay in shape? How do you find the time to dedicate to your body and keep yourself in the best shape possible?" The answer is, it's my #1 priority and one of the reasons that after I became a coach it became one of my specialty areas: health and fitness coaching.

In 1990 I was at a crossroads. I was working in two high-profile positions. I had successfully merged my two careers: sport's television and professional lecture agent into one focus, empowering people to create tangible results through the powerful vehicle of coaching.

Through coaching and training, people can learn how to transform themselves into powerful individuals, discover their passion, and maintain balance in their personal and professional lives.

Twenty-five years training to became a Professional Certified Coach (PCC) certified by (ICF). I am living my dream career as an Executive Life Coach, Facilitator, and Mentor, training and traveling throughout Asia, Europe, and America with the ACTP and ASCTH programs, both accredited by ICF.

My proudest day was my union with Chérie in 1993. I found that having a healthy relationship with myself was the perfect foundation to helping others. I have brought my experiences in health and fitness in sustaining a 26-year soul-mate connection in to my coaching practice to support executives in managing family demands, and in achieving work life balance.

My favorite hobbies are running, photography, golf, cycling, flying single-engine airplanes as an instrument-rated pilot, and enjoying Advanced Open Water Diving.

Healthy activities include conditioning with a passion through golfing, cycling, and transitioning from 10K's up to longer races, marathons. I would never ask of my clients to push their limits if I myself wasn't willing to go there.

Working in Thailand since 2010, I am making a difference in executive's lives through coaching and training.

Defining Culture

Culture is the collection of values, learned beliefs, and behavioral dictates that are shared within a group of people that is self-sustaining and transfers these paradigms from generation to generation. Culture is typically defined as, ways of living, behavioral norms and expectations, language and linguistic expressions, styles of communication, patterns of thinking, beliefs, and values of a particular group. A culture may include shared language, folklore, ideas, thinking patterns, concepts held in common, communication styles, and accepted "truths" held sacred by members of the group.

Frequently, culture plays a greater role in determining communication behavior than race, ethnicity or other Diversity factors and can be what creates conflicts because of differences in perception, orientation, beliefs, and communication styles associated with those cultures. Some facts are:

- Culture determines attitudes and behaviors
- Most cultural norms and rules are assumed and not formally written down
- People's behaviors are interpreted through each person's cultural filter
- No human being is "culture-exempt."

Building relationships is essential for doing business.

There is a complex expectation of respect and building relationships before conducting business; this patience along with practicing emotional restraint are values that coaches are likely to encounter when they begin coaching in Thailand.

Coach and client need to agree on how they would work and what they need to achieve in there initial chemistry session. This relationship between coach and client should develop a sense of rapport, and collaboration in the beginning sessions since each person brings their own beliefs, behaviors, and values to the coaching relationship. They both need to work together and understand that both bring their own various cultures to the table.

It is important to remember not to have your personal culture and overlay influence the session with the client. You need to come in as unbiased, non-judgmental and open-minded.

Business relationships develop slowly in Asia and require time and patience. Establishing a coaching contract may take several meetings with the sponsor, or with the sponsor and the client together over weeks or even months to create a successful business understanding about the purpose and potential outcomes of a coaching relationship. Building long-term relationships is essential in Thailand.

Thai History

Thailand was previously known as the country of Siam, and many people became acquainted with the culture through the musical and film, The King and I. The signature of King Mongkut, King of the Siamese, gave the name "Siam" official status until June 23rd, 1939 when it was finally changed to Thailand. The history of Thailand is long and complex and warrants much more attention than I can allocate in this short chapter.

Thai Religion

One of the most important cultural influencers in the Thai culture is Buddhism. Nearly 95% of the population is Theravada Buddhist. This form of Buddhism is supported and overseen by the government, with monks receiving a number of governmental benefits. As a deeply Buddhist people, Thais place great emphasis on the outward forms of courtesy. Being self-effacing, modest, not embarrassing or intruding on others is an essential part of Thai culture.

Know your place and like it

This is one of the qualities of Buddhism that permeates all aspects of the Thai culture. As a visitor to Thailand, it appears as if people are content with their lot in life and bear no resentment toward others who have more resources at their disposal, which still permeates the countryside. This can also create conflict in a coaching relationship in which the coach is encouraging the client to look at their ideal desired future. The Thai executive may experience tension between their cultural dictates which state, "Know your place and like it!" which also means "Be grateful for what you have!" verses look deep within and see what you really want. The difference in mindset is important to address since accepting your lot in life is antithetical to going for what you really want.

In everyday life in Thailand, there is a strong emphasis on the concept of "sanuk," meaning fun. Because of this, Thais can be quite playful at work and during day-to-day activities, which can be interpreted as "Playing on the job" by those who are not familiar with the culture. This concept of "sanuk" fits nicely with the coaching premise that you can have a life that is satisfying, fulfilling, financially rewarding, and fun.

One automotive Expat executive was focused on results, and one day was encouraged to have more "sanuk," which shocked her. She brought this up in our coaching conversation as an objective: "How can I be results-driven and have more fun at the same time?" The outcome of the session was her determination to assess each situation and sort into three virtual baskets: "Urgent," "Important," and "When time permits." She discovered that she had been reacting to every situation with her "Urgent" response mechanism, and making this adjustment made her more aware, shifted her mindset, and enabled her to have more fun on the job.

Often, Thais will deal with disagreements, minor mistakes, or misfortunes by using the phrase "mai pen rai," translated as "No worries." A smile and the sentence "mai pen rai" communicates that the incident "isn't" no big deal", and therefore there is no conflict or shame involved. When coaching Expats in Thailand who are results-driven, it is useful for the coach to understand how the foreigner's behavior may be perceived, and to shed some light on the cultural differences and perceptions. Feedback can be ideal for engaging in a helpful and learning conversation.

Thii Tam Thii Soong means that people should behave and treat other people according to their own and other people's status. The words literally mean Low place (class) or high place (class) and pertain to age, and family background.

It can be a challenge for younger people to "coach up"- older or more senior people. Senior people look to their peers or even more senior advisors and coaches. Younger coaches often feel intimidated by the seniority of a person with stature, experience, or a significant title on his or her business card. This is a part of the culture that must be addressed if a young coach is to grow his or her coaching practice. This doesn't mean that anyone in their twenties cannot coach anyone older; what it does mean is that this is a delicate situation that must be addressed with sensitivity and appropriateness.

Our Thai company, Motivation Coaching Service, Ltd has graduated many young Thai coaches in their twenties. Part of our success is that we set our course standards high enough so they graduate with confidence, a positive attitude and coaching esteem. They have done the work and know who they are as coaches and believe they'll bring value to executives of all ages.

Sam Ruam is related to the Buddhist concept of moderation, "to travel the middle path." Sam Ruam is about striving to exercise restraint, to maintain composure in stressful situations, and to avoid extreme displays of emotion. There are times in the coaching relationship where the coach is encouraging the client to stand up, speak up, and express his or her feelings.

With the concept of Sam Ruam, the value is restraint not full self-expression. The conflict in this situation would result in the client being non-responsive and caught between two separate values: the traditional Thai behavioral expectations and the urging of the present-day coach. The coaching client who has been let go from his job and feels hurt, angry, confused, lost is reticent to express his feelings since that would not be Sam Ruam, or exercising restraint. When coaching a terminated Thai, you can encourage him or her to share their feelings, however, keep in mind Sam Ruam may keep them in their mind rather than readily exploring their feelings.

"Jai" in Thai language supported by Coaching

Jai means heart, mind, or spirit. There are literally 743 "jai" words in the Thai language. The word jai is combined with other words to create the feeling of an emotion; words that describe emotions or feelings generally end with jai. Through the jai words, one can perceive how consciousness is shaped along with the range of Thai states of mind and emotions.

Below are three "Jai words" for your initial reference to coaching.

Hen Jai is empathy, understanding, or the willingness to listen, be flexible and humane. Hen means to see and you already know that jai means heart. So the literal translation of hen jai is to see into another's heart. In coaching, hen Jai is a essential since empathy is required in coaching, and should be addressed as a way to build relationships and especially cultural bridges between the coach and the Thai culture. Demonstrating hen jai enhances the coaching relationship.

Wai jai means starting to trust someone. In the past there may have been issues that created reticence or doubt. That reluctance has now been replaced with trust, which is absolutely fundamental in coaching. If your coaching client says they have wai jai with you, it means that they believe you have their best interests in your heart. Wai jai is a wonderful compliment, so when you hear it accept it graciously.

Greng-Jai refers to a person restraining his/her intentions if there is the potential for discomfort, inconvenience, or potential conflict with another. The word greng literally means fear. In this context, the fear is about making another uncomfortable.

Greng-jai is deeply embedded in the Thai culture. You need to know about greng-jai because it could be at a block to supportive direct questioning and interpreted as confrontation creating discomfort. Asking powerful questions encourages the client to go deeper and look at his or her preferences, choices, awareness, perceptions, and behavior patterns in relation to their desired future.

Greng Jai has many interpretations. For example, the hesitation to ask questions when you haven't understood someone, the reluctance to provide feedback for another especially when it's not positive, or encouraging your client to stand up for him/herself when it might inconvenience or cause another discomfort might create a disconnect between coach and client.

All of these are examples of Greng-Jai. Greng-Jai can make coaching more challenging since many of the greng-Jai behaviors are antithetical to the expectations in the coaching relationship. When you are conducting a chemistry session/meeting with a new client, it is best to address greng-jai upfront and discuss how it might impact your coaching relationship… and if it does, encourage your client to say, "This is a greng-jai moment, how shall we best address it?"

Ms. Bee is an Executive Assistant to the Managing Director. She has made previous plans to pick up her daughter after school to celebrate her good grades. A few minutes before departing, her boss walks in to her office and tells her to drop him off at his business appointment in the opposite directions from where she was going. This conflicting request places her in the grip of greng-jai and according to Thai culture; she will need to postpone her celebration with her daughter.

Thai Concepts Practiced in Business

Hai Kiad means to give honor and respect. This important principle is in complete alignment with core coaching competencies like building trust and intimacy, partnering with the client, and active listening. Therefore, Hai Kiad is fundamental to the coaching relationship in Thailand. You can use it in your initial chemistry coaching session.

Katanyu rookhun translates into gratitude and indebtedness. The executive holds this obligation or duty toward his/her parents, guardians, teachers, caretakers, mentors, and bosses. It describes the feelings and practices involved in relationships. In a coaching relationship, the Thai executive stated, "This is what will please my parents," or "This is what will make my parents proud when they tell their friends about my career." This conflict is seen as a double bind. "Can I please my parents (since I owe them Katanyu rookhun), and at the same time honor my own preferences?"

While western culture is known to emphasize individuality, the Thai culture, like many other Asian cultures, is a collectivist one. Thais are raised to naturally focus outwardly – to always think about how one is expected to behave in others' eyes in certain situations. When asked, "what do you want to do," the client may answer from the place of "wanting to do what is expected in order to be deemed appropriate and kind." With cultural understanding and respect, a coach can empathetically understand that desire to please, and gently encourage the client to find his or her own voice and preferences.

As a coach who embraces diversity, the coach has to distance himself from his personal attitudes and culture. If the client wants to deviate from his culture, the coach must find out who will be impacted by his decision.

In a Thai family business, the transition from Son to Manager to Leader is also about finding one's true voice and not simply doing what one is told to do.

Mr. Satin wanted to excel, but all of his cultural dictates advised him to blend in and harmonize. When his father approached him about heading up the family business, he basically held his breath.

He envisioned accommodating 40 individuals with differing agendas, and being caught in the middle of every decision.

He felt very uncomfortable but found that he couldn't speak up. The pressure was overwhelming and his guilt of even considering that he didn't want to do this was enormous.

The inner conflict was the focus of our coaching sessions. His specific objective was, "How can I communicate my wishes to my father in such a way that he understands what I want and supports my wishes and my choices?"

Before the Thai client made his decisions in the session he had to sort out, how his ideas would affect the family business and who needed to be considered in this decision.

When coaching abroad, it is important to understand how to use the culture as a connector. You need to be fully aware of the cultural concepts that may conflict with coaching principles.

Acknowledging assumptions, cultural norms, and expectations on the table helps to open up the conversation to go to a deeper and more authentic level.

Expats working in Asia must be sensitive that their own culture doesn't overly influence how they manage their Thai teams.

It is important in Thailand to allocate quality time in getting to know your clients as a prelude to conducting business.

Living and working in Asia as an executive life coach has taught me to adapt to my client's cultural dictates. It is necessary to distance my culture so we can learn together. Coaching is a partnership where the client feels the safety to move forward creating their ideal outcomes and goals.

My mission has provided me with fulfillment as I continue to help my clients across the globe realize their dreams!

Reference materials:
Holmes, Henry, and Tangtongtavy, Suchada. ©1995. *Working with the Thais*. White Lotus. Bangkok, Thailand
Dr. Cherie Carter-Scott, MCC & Lynn U. Stewart, PCC - *Transformational Life Coaching* ©2007 Health Communications, Inc., FL, USA

Kate Gardner

Kate Gardner is a #1 International Best-Selling Author, Editor in Chief of The Missing Piece Magazine and Publisher of the International Best-Selling Book Series The Missing Piece. As coach Kate helps raise her client's self-esteem and self-confidence through providing marketing tools and platforms to help them present themselves to highly targeted traffic.

CHAPTER 14

SOCIAL MEDIA SHAPES & FORMS THE WORLD

Kate Gardner

When I set out on my journey to become a life coach over 4 years ago, I never thought in a million years I would have the immense journey that I have. I thought I would totally rock it with all my 8 years' business experience from running a really successful childcare business offline. How WRONG! Was I? I was completely wrong!

The online industry was completely different in every sense and it was a whole new world that I had to learn. I had to start over and completely re-educate myself in sales, marketing, copywriting, leadership, personal growth and technical skills.

The world we live in is constantly changing and we need to keep up with the constant change or we will be left behind. I have experienced this myself in the online industry as a business owner if you don't keep polishing your skills in modern day then you will get left behind.

Industries are constantly changing and adapting to new modern ways of doing things and the consumer needs to constantly learn new ways of how to work modern technology in order to stay connected to the people in their lives and to socialised in their social circle. Gone are the days where many people use to chat face to face and instead they can send an instant message to somebody who lives 60,000 miles away from them and receive an instant reply in seconds.

Professional bodies and service providers also require continuing training and education due to the fast change in certain laws. They need to be educated frequently on what requirements are needed to stay in certain guidelines within the services they provide or the people they work with. Agreements have to be written and continuous learning in this area could save issues further down the line. Disclaimers have to be published on the 2nd page of any author's book to protect them from any reader taking legal action against them if the information was not stated from a personal experience in the first place.

With bringing all this to light it definitely shows that in today's modern society we have to take more responsibility and start to become fully aware of placing solid foundations down to begin with and incorporate a way of continued education in our lives in order to stay fully aware of the changing world around us.

Nobody likes to be left behind or have their dreams shattered 6 months later when they find out the way something is carried out now, is not the way it will be done 6 months later and results in landing them in hot water because they didn't take the time to educate themselves in the first place. I have learnt many hard lessons on my journey to success and I learnt that by taking longer to prepare stronger foundations before setting out on any project actually saved me a whole lot of failure and money down the road.

I hope by sharing 3 specific tips that include action steps and examples, I can really help you on your way to succeeding online with your business.

1. Get Some Rules Written

One of the biggest fears of starting out in an online business and something that worries us human beings on a daily basis is what other people think about us. Until your confidence grows in yourself as a business owner, there will be times when this fear can lead to desperation of wanting everybody to like you so that your business becomes successful.

The pitfalls of this is that we can attract unwanted attention from people who just wish to sit around and want to chat all day on social media and attract clients that make you want to rip your hair out in frustration. The whole purpose of this book is to help you and stop you making the same mistakes as we did. I myself worked from that same desperation at one time in my business. It was one of the biggest reasons my first ever book project failed on a worldwide level.

The book project stalled because no people were signing up to the project. The project launch date had to be placed back twice and the desperation of jumping on every Tom, Dick, and Harry that joined my friends list set in.

The desperation led me to sit around and chatting to dead leads through social media in the hope that they would sign up to the project. It pushed my health and mental state to the brink. I had to admit failure, which was like a punch in the stomach.

I had to go back to the drawing board and start from scratch with the project and spend more time and money to correct what was not working. The title, concept, and mission of the book were transformed. I changed the book title to The Missing Piece: A Transformational Journey and re-launched into the world and the makeover attracted the people it needed to make this book a complete success.

When we launched the book on December the 7th 2013, it went straight to #1 on the Amazon Best Sellers charts. I was completely gob smacked! I had made my very public failure become a worldwide success and now it was time for me to serious, get my act together because I was now going to be seen as a, "Go to Expert". This is exactly what a best-selling author title does for you, it makes people sit up and take notice of you, and a book is an amazing powerful marketing tool. That is the reason why I write so many and will continue to do so, plus I love writing as well.

Now that I had the platform, I had to get serious with myself and my business. I started writing policies for my business and had certain standards. In return, this started to attract paying clients and my business was now making a profit.

I always advise any business owner to write polices and disclaimers FIRST! If you have a rule book to begin with, it will save you a whole lot of stress, frustration, and heartbreak down the line. Take it from somebody who experienced it and I really do not want you to feel that either. I am going to share with you one of my templates that I used on a daily basis with my social media inbox at the beginning of my "expert" journey.

I want you to save time and ditch the time wasters from the beginning. It's rather easy to separate the time wasters in your inbox to the real leads to a sale with just one message. The person's reaction to the message you send will instantly tell you if they are a willing to do business with you or if they are just a social media chatter box, who only does just that, chat. You can use this template exactly if you like and place your own details in the bank areas.

Hello [NAME}
Great to connect with you today!
Wishing you much success with your 2016 and everything you do. Please do not hesitate to reach out to me if you need help with [WHATEVER YOUR SERVICE IS]. You can check out my services at [PUT WEB ADDRESS HERE]
Please note that I only chat to followers through my Facebook business page at [PUT BIZ PAGE LINK HERE] where I will be happy to engage with you and reply to all your comments.
In the meantime, I wish you much love and gratitude and thank you so much for connecting with me today. I look forward to helping you with {WHATEVER SERVICE YOU PROVIDE] [IF YOU OFFER 30 MIN FREE CONSULTATIONS, THEN PLACE THE OFFER HERE]
Much Love & Gratitude

Now I want to also share with you some great tips so that you can sell your products and services online easily. Raising our self-confidence is the key to helping you work from a place of self-respect, rather than a place of desperation.

2. Effective Communication

Building a successful business is all about building relationships with people. Gone are the days of cold-calling to make your business a success. People hate cold-callers!

There is nothing more uncomfortable than dealing with cold-callers. People will not part with their cash unless they trust you and your brand.

Friending your followers is extremely important. Remember, behind their computers, each and every follower of yours is a human being just like you, and they have families and interests. They also come with their own friends lists of 250—5,000+ people, which means that these people could very well become your clients too.

How you speak to everyone online is really going to have an effect on your credibility as an online business owner.

Communication is key when you start to engage with your following. The way you communicate tells the world everything! Every email, message, and post you send out to the world tells everything about your personality and emotions at the time of writing it.If you are sad or annoyed, then this will come across to everyone who reads it unless you are highly aware of how you are communicating.

You should only write to your following with one thing in mind. Write to them like you truly love them and that love will come across, leaving the reader to feel the love from your words.

Whatever is happening within our subconscious minds determines the outcomes that are projected from us. We have no control over this because to us, our emotions are completely normal. The habits and beliefs we have are our normality. I know when I read a message or post from someone; I am reading their emotional state of mind at that time along with their words.

This is why communication is so important to your business. You want to reply to your clients and following from a place of love. These people are extremely important to you, and if it was not for them, you would not have a business that earns.

Your clients and following need to know how important they are. When it comes to writing your social media posts, please take into account that this will bring across to the world the person you truly are and will determine your credibility as a business owner. There are many pairs of eyes reading your posts day in day out. Over 900 million people use Facebook each day. Whatever you post and one person likes, then that person has just shared it with their following also. Your post will show up in their friends' news feeds, which opens you up another list of people containing anything from 250-5,000 members.

How you represent yourself in your posts is vital. Your words and how you write them give away everything about you. If you are a caring and loving person, this will come across to the following and they will connect with this instantly, which will attract the right people to you. These people are your potential clients and will turn into great people to work with.

Just Remember:
"Don't be afraid to display your personality, just always be aware of doing it in a professional and inspiring manner."

3. Market like it's 2017

Marketing is something in the online world of business that has changed massively in the past 4 years alone. No longer do people fall for the "How to make 6 figures in 6 hours" bullshit that has been rammed down their throats for far too long.

We live in a mobile world and if you are not marketing like it is 2017 (yes be ahead of the game) and learning how to create a like, know and trust factor and present yourself the right way through a mobile device to your following, then you will miss out my friend.

Your audience wants to know you are human so they don't feel they have to live up to a huge expectation that they could possibly not deliver. They need to hear it from you that you have failed, that you have had shitty moments on your journey to success and they need to know the solutions you can provide. When a person who follows you learns that your life was not a bed of roses, a whole relief washes over them.
Suddenly it motivates them to know that yippee!!! If she/he did this, THEN SO CAN I!

Now, don't get me wrong there is a line drawn to what you do place out to the world and nobody wants to know what colour underwear you are wearing, nor do they wish to see your bathroom selfie while you are doing your toilet business, but what they do want to see is your vulnerable side as well as your powerhouse side.

They want to see you in everyday life sharing everyday things and see rich content delivery that will help them jump the hurdles of doubt, frustration and hair pulling moments. in return, you will build amazing relationships and build your business on strong foundations that will lead to providing a service for centuries to come.

It is your job as a service provided to stay on top of your game and always be learning, researching and understanding what the custom is sick of seeing, and learn what goes on in their minds and understand what they want to see. What are their needs? Wants? Desires?

This journey is not about us, it is about what we can do for others and the greatest way we can build strong deeper meaningful relationships with people is to open ourselves up and become human and show our human side.

If we keep talking about ourselves and what we have achieved and not consider how people feel and think, then It won't work for you, it will lead you nowhere fast and it will make your customer feel like they are just an ATM machine at your service for a one-time payment. Human beings need to know they are cared for and the only thing that will help your business succeed is if you market like you give a shit.

It's not hard to do and you can bring your own feelings across in many ways like:
- Podcasting
- Live video through Facebook
- Video blogs
- Radio shows
- Internet TV shows
- Written blogs
- E books
- Paperback books
- Building communities
- Creating culture on a public level (See my Facebook profile for the worldwide video challenge)
- Facebook pages

However you to choose to bring yourself across to the world, just remember to understand people and love them.

Christy Whitman

Christy Whitman is a transformational leader, abundance coach and the New York Times bestselling author of two books, including *The Art of Having It All*. She has appeared on The Today Show and The Morning Show and her work has been featured in People Magazine, Seventeen, Woman's Day, Hollywood Life, and Teen Vogue, among others. As the CEO and founder of the Quantum Success Learning Academy & the Quantum Success Coaching Academy, a 12-month Law of Attraction coaching certification program, Christy has helped thousands of people worldwide to achieve their goals through her empowerment seminars, speeches, and coaching sessions and products. Her life-changing message reaches over 200,000 people a month and her work has been promoted by and featured with esteemed authors and luminaries such as Marianne Williamson, Dr. Wayne Dyer, Marci Shimoff, Brian Tracy, Neale Donald Walsch, Abraham-Hicks, and Louise Hay. She currently lives in Montreal with her husband, Frederic, and their two boys, Alexander and Maxim.

CHAPTER 15

"LAW OF ATTRACTION" COACHING

Christy Whitman

What is Law of Attraction Coaching, and how does it differ from other coaching methods?

The most significant difference between Law of Attraction coaching and other life coaching methods is that it is founded on the understanding that everything in the universe, including ourselves, is made of energy, and all energy resonates at a particular frequency, or vibration. As Law of Attraction coaches, we teach our clients how to create their experience deliberately and on purpose, by becoming conscious of the energy or frequency they are offering in relation to each important aspect of their lives.

It's important to acknowledge that the phenomenon that is now understood as the Law of Attraction is far from new. In fact, this universal law has been written about and passed down throughout the ages by wisdom traditions all over the world. When Buddha made the observation that "As a man thinketh, so he becomes," he was conveying the essence of this powerful law. Even the Golden Rule, which advises us to "Do unto others as we would have others do unto us" is a testament to the basic understanding that we can only reap what we have sewn, and what we send out eventually comes back.

In practical terms, the Law of Attraction teaches us that the energy we offer or broadcast – not just through our actions, but through the thoughts, feelings, and beliefs that we generate in the invisible realm of our inner world – eventually manifests into outer form. Everything we manifest in our external world, including the state of our bodies, our relationships, our finances, are a direct reflection of the frequency we are offering.

The Law of Attraction is a universal phenomenon, meaning it works for everyone, all the time, whether we are aware of it or not. And just like the law of gravity, once our clients understand how it works, they can stop unwittingly fighting against it and start using it to their greatest benefit.

Most clients seek out life coaching because they desire to effect a change in one or more circumstances of their lives. Unlike traditional life coaching, where the goal is to help clients improve those conditions by working at the level of form, Law of Attraction coaching works at the level of energy. And while there is some variance in the methodology used by individual LOA coaches, most follow a basic formula that is similar to the one I use to train the coaches who become certified through my Quantum Success Coaching Academy: Clarity + Alignment + Action = Manifestation.

Anytime we experience something we don't want – a failure in business, for example, or a breakdown in an important relationship – we automatically gain greater clarity about what we do want. Like most coaches, our first order of business is to support our clients in creating a clear vision of what it is they desire. What sets Law of Attraction coaching apart is that once our clients have clarified this vision, we offer countless tools to support them in aligning themselves – in thought, belief, emotion and action – with that vision. As clients make the correlation between what they think, what they feel, and what they ultimately attract into their lives, they begin to understand that they hold the key to manifesting anything they desire.

Does working with the Law of Attraction mean all we have to do is visualize what we want and it will 'magically' appear?

Not at all. There is no 'magic' pill, and anything we desire to create requires some degree of action. However, when we understand the Law of Attraction, we learn to leverage our actions to achieve more with less effort by ensuring that we are acting from an internal state of clarity and alignment. Most coaching methods advocate motivation techniques – creating consequences and rewards around attaining goals, for example

– as a way of compelling their clients to take action. As Law of Attraction coaches, we support our clients in achieving their goals through taking inspired actions – the impulses, intuitive nudges and ideas that arise naturally when we're connected to the essence of what we desire.

Action that is taken without the clarity and focus that comes from alignment is not only exhausting; it's actually counterproductive. If you've ever attempted to do something and felt like you were "running in circles," or "taking one step forward and two steps back," you've experienced firsthand that motion by itself does not equal motion forward. What creates forward progress is the power that only focus can bring.

Actions that are fueled by a state of internal alignment have a momentum behind them that can literally magnetize miracles into our lives. Law of Attraction coaching teaches clients how to infuse their outer actions with greater power through internal processes such as intending, visualizing, aligning and allowing. Said another way, we show them the power of deliberately deciding how they want to feel, and getting into that state of being before they do anything. As clients learn to bring clarity and alignment in each important area of their lives, they begin to witness manifestations that unfold with much greater ease.

A few minutes of aligning our energy with the outcome we want to create is far more powerful than hours and hours of action taken without this connection. It's like the difference between using an electronic device that is running on battery power versus one that is plugged in and being fully charged by a live electrical current. Action that is infused with energy and intention produces results that are astonishing compared to what can be accomplished with action alone.

What types of goals can a Law of Attraction coach help me to achieve?

Because the Law of Attraction is a universal principle, understanding how to apply it will support you in achieving your goals in virtually every aspect of your life – whether your desire is to create more success in business, generate greater financial abundance, enjoy better relationships with those around you, or simply to feel more confident and at ease within yourself.

The ultimate goal of a Law of Attraction coach is to support our clients in becoming more attuned to the vibration they are offering in any moment, and this usually involves some retraining, because most of us have been taught to prioritize others' needs above our own, and are accustomed to habitually reacting to the circumstances around us rather than deliberately choosing our response to life. Learning to redirect our focus within ourselves is a skill that we have to develop, but this is key to understanding – and therefore mastering – our own energy field.

By teaching our clients how to read and redirect their own energy, we give them access to an inner compass that they can take into every aspect of their lives and into each new situation. Once they've achieved this mastery, they no longer need a coach; they have their own internal guidance to rely on.

Jami and Marla Keller founded Passion Provokers in 2011 after they had spent the previous 21 years working in the coaching field. Many patterns emerged in this field, and they soon realized they needed to rebrand what it meant to have and to be in relationships. Jami and Marla Keller became Relationship Coaches and Licensed Facilitators with Life Skills International in 1995. From personal trials to professional success, they resolved to give everyone outstanding success in their relationship goals.

Their coaching is short-term (a maximum of 12 months) for a lifetime of results. With their unique way of coaching together, Jami and Marla have created simple teachings and processes that empower their clients to discover their passions and begin living into them. Since their job is to empower people's lives and evoke a passion to thrive, they realized "provoking passion" was their job; hence, the name evolved into Passion Provokers.

CHAPTER 16

POWER FROM PAIN

Jami and Marla Keller

My husband, Jami, and I love being Relationship Coaches! And there isn't anything we ask our clients to do that we are not, or have not, already done in our own lives. Some of the things we recommend we have mastered, and some we are still mastering. Being human is part of being a coach. But that's okay because being a few steps ahead feels reachable.

There are two things that would have helped us most when we started coaching as a couple twenty-one years ago. First, that pain is central to any area of coaching. What we have found consistently is that it is an outdated reaction to the pain of life that people need coaching for whether the goal is financial, personal, or relational. Helping clients discover and cope with this pain is the key to coaching in general.

And second, the key to building a successful coaching practice is reaching your niche audience. One of our biggest struggles has been marketing. We have poured money into advertising in all medias—radio (we did a weekly morning clip, answering questions from inquiring minds about all things relational), magazines, newspapers, etc. We may have gotten one client from the radio, a big "0" from the others. We do have to say the networking groups have had a bit better success. We've had around twelve clients from networking. The thing that we had to decide was if the money and time we were putting in to each group was worth it. One thing has worked. You would probably never guess what it is - Super Fans. In the second part of our chapter we will share what took us years to discover: how to find, connect, and communicate well with our "Super Fans," and the key to future clients from current and past clients.

FIRST "What Hurts?"

We have always worked with people to find, build, and heal love. Long before we knew that we were coaching people, friends and strangers would end up hanging out late into a Saturday night telling us about their deepest, often secret pain. The one constant in every person who is seeking help, and this is everyone we've coached, is pain. Do you know what it took to become sought-after coaches? Dealing with our own shit. Yes, even if you are in the business sector. When I (Marla) was first trained as a Facilitator and Coach for Life Skills International in 1995 I knew I had it all together, and was being trained altruistically to help others. Because I had those skills. And because my family was perfect. How sweet… I learned pretty fast (third day of training—not fast enough!) that I had issues. I do have to give myself some love since I was 27 and thought I knew pretty much everything. Pride comes before something…what was it. Oh, yes, a fall.

And our coupleship experienced an epic fall. You can read more about it on our website at PassionProvokers.com, and as you can see we are here. But we didn't get here without feeling the pain, processing through it, and creating healthy boundaries. This is why couples in crisis come to us. We've been there, and we know that almost everything is fixable if our coaching guidance is followed.

There is no way around it. Pain is real and how we deal with it matters, more than we ever thought. Top social science researcher, Brené Brown, agrees with us in her newest book, Rising Strong. In it she says, "The opposite of recognizing that we're feeling something is denying our emotions. The opposite of being curious is disengaging. When we deny our stories and disengage from tough emotions, they don't go away; instead, they own us, they define us." Boom.

We have always done two things to help a client move through their pain, and those two very important things are naming the pain and then forgiving the pain (along with those around it). And this has been highly effective, giving us an outstanding success rate for our clients.

And this is what inspired us create our most popular coaching tool, the Feeling Wheel 4.0, as well as our Feeling Wheel App available at iTunes.

It has gone through several transformations from the time we started learning, and then teaching this idea that feelings are important and need to be expressed back in 1995. At that time, we were introduced to a very meager, blue and white (ditto copied!) feeling wheel that had maybe ½ of the feelings we have on ours and no hub at the center with the foundational feelings you can see on our wheel. And it had been dittoed so many times that both sides had partial words. The hub we created turned out to be the same modes described by neuroscience researcher and author Tara Bennett Goleman in her book Mind Whispering that we drop into within a millisecond when we are triggered. And the core of transformation ended up being forgiveness.

This is why when we tell our clients that we are going to forgive someone to move forward in our process, they almost always say "Oh, I have already done that." And when they journey through it with us they find that they had stuffed it under the rug because it was too painful to look at, and that the rug wouldn't hold any more things to stuff and the result was a place to trip and fall, more pain, and serious relational distress.

The truth is forgiveness is almost never complete. There are people we have forgiven hundreds of times and still have more to do. Some connections are worth doing this to promote healing forward, while other relationships are unhealthy and the forgiveness is simply for us or our client's hearts to be more vulnerable, connected and open in the relationships that matter. And so that they can have better boundaries with toxic people. Forgiveness always leads to more truth, which inevitably leads to healthy boundaries.

By the time we are seven-years-old we have learned 90% or so of everything we will ever learn in our lifetime, therefore it makes sense that not revisiting how we actually learned (or didn't learn) to process things like forgiveness in our childhood will create problems in our adulthood.

Here's the bottom line: our old habits that have become totally unconscious to us begin to defeat us. Just like brushing our teeth in the morning we do things like "forgiveness" without thinking about what we are doing or how we feel about it. So those childish ways of dealing with things remain. We have all seen an adult meltdown demonstrate a temper tantrum... Not a good look for anyone.

The tricky thing is that it most often works, or at least gives us a dependable result even if that result is killing relationships.

So we naturally dug into forgiveness as well as connecting an ability to feel the pain of what is broken, hurt, neglected and connect that pain to a person, event or place in order to forgive healthfully and develop a new boundary.

And the reason we have spent the last few pages on this is that it is vital to understand and practice consistently as a coach. What we see most often, as a mistake new coaches make, is not practicing the skills that are being coached. This results in the triggering strong feelings of pain in the coach, and there are all kinds of things that can go wrong when this happens.

Our very best tool is awareness. Good coaches are empathic and have sorted out their feelings so that when they are NOT triggered by a clients' issues or behavior, they do not give into the temptation to cause pain to the client where they have been hurt before. Just being aware of this subtle temptation is vital to coaching well. This takes accountability and coaching for you... PLEASE DO NOT SKIMP IN THIS AREA if you intend to lead others.

Forgiveness turns out to be the most powerful tool we use for our clients and ourselves. It is also a very specific skill that requires much practice in order to teach without being overwhelmed. Forgiveness requires us to be present to the pain or we get stuck. Very stuck. If you are stuck growing your coaching practice, dig into forgiveness in and around the places where things are not working well, process through it, and watch things begin to flow.

Beginning with feelings and relating to them healthfully is how you will start taking your power back, and continue using your power for the talents and strengths that are your natural gifts.

At PassionProvokers.com we have the Forgiveness Booklet where we profile how to fully forgive and grieve in what is really the shortest shortcut. Any shorter and you would be standing still, and any additions to what we teach often lead to confusion! Why not stick with what we have found to work 100% of the time after coaching 1000's of clients?

This is not for the faint of heart, and if you are not willing to feel your pain, and we mean really feel it, stop coaching now. It takes an emotional badass to fully be present and open to the power that pain gives each and every one of us. That is only if we are willing to be brave enough to feel it, allow it to be real, and make the best choices in how we express it.

As coaches it is our job to guide our clients to become aware of their blind spots, and teach them to use tools to gain more awareness and effectiveness as a result. Again, this art form of leading people through breakthroughs requires that we do not let our pain get in the way. And let's face it, as coaches we are human, and pain does not happen on a schedule around your client's needs. Your readiness to deal with your own and your client's needs is akin to being a lifeguard. Be careful of jumping into "dangerous water" without the right tools.

FINDING AND DEVELOPING YOUR TARGET AUDIENCE

When you have done the above with success, you will find the next step of your coaching practice is finding and developing your target audience. This we found is done through your Super Fans. Super Fans are easy to identify. They are the people, other than your mom, who like and share everything you post and believe in your true mission.

Once you have three or four of them the key is to do a good profiling of them. By age, economic status, gender, religion, Geographics, and introversion/extroversion.

The last criteria can be self-reported knowing that there are three main types when it comes to brain alertness levels (the core of introversion vs. extroversion) and those are extreme introvert, balanced and extreme extrovert. This is important in terms of how they might like to be engaged.

You don't even really need to talk to them much to figure these things out. Most of this can be deducted by things you already know by observation. Once you have a solid profile of who your Super Fans are you can begin to use this information for targeting future clients.

Marketing is the elusive magic. Especially when we as coaches are nurturing our clients to be independent. Coaching needs to be short-term with refreshers annually, and with each client we ought to be working ourselves out of a job whenever possible. We want our clients to experience freedom when they are finished with our sessions so that they will go out and conquer their world. Super Fan created!

When a Coach is doing a good job the client learns how to deal with their pain independently and also know's how to help someone who is ready find the coach that will work for them.

Serving your clients in their deepest pain, guiding them through that pain, and experiencing the deep peace, empowerment and joy that they begin to live into is what makes you a great coach. And before you can offer that guidance to your client, you will need to be living in it yourself. Simply dive in to the tools above and you will not only change your world, but you will create a movement that will change our world for the better one client at a time.

Liza Boubari, CCHt, CSMc

Liza Boubari, CCHt, CSMc, is a Clinical Hypnotherapist and Stress Management Consultant who currently sits on the Executive Board of the American Council of Hypnotherapy Examiners (ACHE). In the last twenty-five years there has been a growing interest in the connection between the mind and body and its relationship to stress and disease. Liza's knowledge of the corporate world is due to years of experience in law offices as a paralegal and legal assistant. It was her own powerful healing experience through hypnotherapy that led her to this science. Changing course, she chose this path to help others. In 1997 she founded HealWithin, Inc., a Healing Center for Mind-Body Therapy - and has since been expanding her practice in her community. Liza has published three manuals "Heal-Thy Mind-Body", "Stand Up to Slim Down", and "Stomp on Smoking", which are now available on Amazon.com. She is well known for her innovative 3E Event, seminars and workshops on stress management, and the mind-body connection. Liza's website is: www.HealWithin.com
818-551-1501

CHAPTER 17

3E - EVOKE, EMBRACE, EVOLVE

Liza Boubari, CCHt, CSMc

Evoke your passion and let go of the past.
Embrace your femininity and accept the now.
Evolve spiritually and bring forth what you desire in the future.

You have taken the first step toward your personal journey. Hypnotherapy opens your mind's deepest reservoir to bringing change and the power to heal within.

Do you know what you stand for – what you feel or want to be and do that you consider fulfilling?

As a child I knew I wanted to be of help and service to others. I was aware of certain values that were important to me, and went through changing four careers and feel blessed to where I am today - embracing the concept of core values and 3E's. Looking back, each career had a direct correlation to helping others – but I was not fully happy until my own experience of healing through hypnotherapy that led me to practice, coach and guide my clients make a positive difference in their life.

Just about everyone has a dream or goal they want to achieve. This is what keeps us motivated and alive. When you feel strongly about making a change or achieving something, you're going to put in the time and energy required to make it happen.
However, what if they could not do it on their own – that's when you come in. You can help by coaching them move towards the finish line. Hypnotherapy might just be the tool that helps them get ahead in their goals working from the inside-out.

Attitude

You are well aware that your attitude determines the overall course of your life and career.

What are you attracting into your life? Why?
Do you surround yourself by negative people who zap your energy or positive folks who empower you? Are they:

- Healthy or unhealthy?
- Respectful or abusive?
- Winners or whiners?
- Kind or critical?
- Givers or takers?
- Successful or destructive?

The people around you define you as a person. You want them to lift you up and enhance your life both personally or professionally. It does matter - because YOU MATTER.

Through the course of my life's journey, I have found that reflecting on who I surround myself with has set the course of my life. We all have gone through life's ups and downs. From good friends and not so good ones, caught up in a routine life or tend to stay put only not to rock the boat.

But how often do you examine how healthy that routine may be? When is it going to be bad enough for you to make a change?

Change happens when one of two elements are present.
1- The pain is so bad that you can no longer stand feeling it,
2- The reward is so great that you can't but want to achieve it.

You can push harder when it comes to achieving your dreams. Have you not dropped weight only to fit in two sizes smaller for the 10th High School reunion? I bet you have!
To become the person that you want to be, you do things that you haven't done before. Break out of your comfort zone and grow as person!

Remember: Attitude is a choice, make yours a positive and vibrate one today!

The Practice of Hypnotherapy

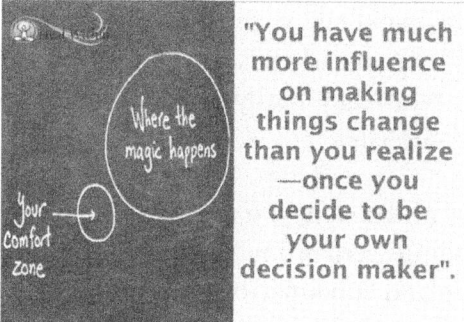

"You have much more influence on making things change than you realize —once you decide to be your own decision maker".

Hypnotherapy is a way of recreating your life story from this moment forward.

Its historical context is familiar to many, with a sense of mysticism. I believe, to be a hypnotherapist one must have an interest in the art and science of the mind, the inner workings of the subconscious mind, as well as a desire to help others make significant and instantaneous changes. It's like opening the chip of a computer to read or edit the code or programing within.

When we are born we are from birth imposed upon with a set of predetermined ideas, thoughts, beliefs, or as I like to refer to them- tapes. We are in a sense hypnotized to live, think, behave, and believe in a certain way imposed on us by our families, teachers, churches and society. These ideas that we have learned early on may not be in any way a reality that will benefit us for the rest of our lives.

Many of these ideas are simply someone else's beliefs imposed on us. We take all of this into our subconscious as truth and often times let this become our belief system for life. These ideas may be positive or negative, true or false but none the less, they have a big influence on who we become and the way we will think about ourselves and impact the outcome of our lives. These outside influences unknowingly program our subconscious mind into believing that which may not be true or healthy for us.

Did you know you can get in touch with your inner being and recreate a healthier and better You? The possibilities are endless. All you need to do to accomplish this is to just imagine what you want, feel it with enthusiasm, and believe it in your heart and hypnosis will take you there.

Desire, belief and expectancy are all you need to change lives through hypnosis. It is so sad that people go through their lives with misconceptions of who they really are and what they could actually become and or accomplish.

As a hypnotherapist and coach, you must attempt to relate to your clients with compassion while remaining objective as they become aware of their inner dialogue and subconscious behaviors and attitudes.
Many people go through life believing these mistruths and remain unhappy and unfulfilled simply because they do not realize they can reprogram their subconscious mind and recreate these unhealthy tapes. This is where you as a coach come in.

This is where you help their inner computer mind be reprogrammed with new healthy fulfilling suggestions and those old unfulfilling stories or tapes removed. Through hypnosis we can get into contact with our subconscious mind and reprogram all those negative false beliefs we have been carrying around with us all of our life.

It seems so true that thoughts are things. What we think about all the time truly does come about.

Thoughts can become reality!

What you think and the words you speak to yourself generate 100 percent of the results you get in life. How you communicate with yourself and others depends entirely on how they understand you. Switch your language and you change the outcome.

People need to realize they have some control over their lives. God gave us a magnificent (conscious and subconscious) mind to use to create our reality through our thoughts and imagination. "So as a man thinketh, so shall he be". So true are these words if we would only pay attention and act on these truths.

Hypnosis can help us to think in positive ways to help us create a new reality which in turn could help create a more positive universe. Just imagine if all people would learn self-hypnosis and reprogram their subconscious mind to live a more rewarding and happy life free of negativity, pain, fears, even drugs. It would help them to accomplish their desires, therefore making it easier to be kinder to others.

Think it and you will. Imagine it and you create. Desire it and you become.

It all begins with self.

If we are individually fulfilled and learn to love ourselves we are much better able to love others as well. If society as a whole were happier with themselves and more fulfilled in their individual lives, they would be less likely be jealous or envious of others. This could cause a decrease in crime and abuse of mankind in general. If we all could only learn how to use what we were all gifted with, which is our subconscious mind, our world could be a better place.

To break patterns of behavior is to stop repeating the same pattern.

The first step is to Evoke what was (to acknowledge that a negative pattern exists). Then, to Embrace what is now (recognize the characteristics that initiate the pattern to be repeated).
Lastly, to Evolve to what is to be (edit or change the patterns for the better).

How does Your Mind work.

The concept of three levels of mind is nothing new. Sigmund Freud, the famous Austrian psychologist was probably the first to popularize it into mainstream society as we know it today. Freud created a useful model of the mind, which he separated into 3 tiers or sections – the conscious mind or ego, the preconscious, and the unconscious mind.
The best way to illustrate the concept of the three minds is by using a triangle.

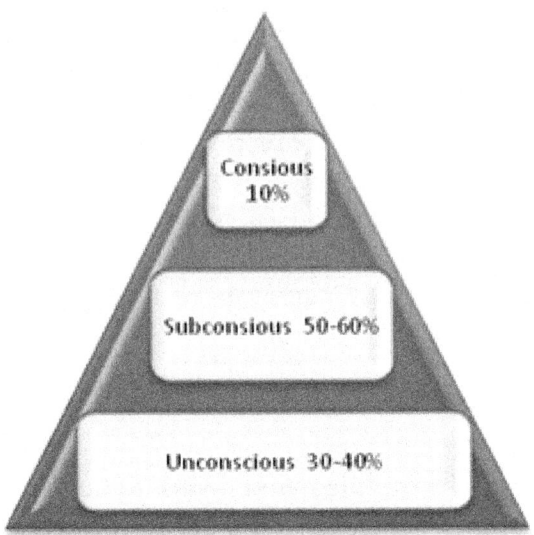

Your conscious mind occupies at the top, representing about 10% of your brain capabilities.

Mid level is a slightly larger section that is referred to as the subconscious. It accounts for around 50-60% of your brain capabilities.

The section below that is the unconscious mind. It occupies the base of the triangle and fills out the other 30-40% of your brain capabilities.

How They Work Together

Your conscious mind is what most people associate with who you are, because that is where most people live day to day. Consciously, you look – listen - learn.
Your conscious mind is the part giving out orders. It communicates to the outside world and the inner self through speech (verbal), pictures (visual), writing, physical movement (Kinesthetic or touch), and thought.

The subconscious mind "stores information, recalls information and regulates your entire bodily functions." It is in charge of your recent memories, and is in continuous contact with the resources of the unconscious mind.

The unconscious mind is the storehouse of all memories and past experiences, both those that have been repressed through trauma and those that have simply been consciously forgotten and no longer important to us. It's from these memories and experiences that our beliefs, habits, and behaviors are formed. The unconscious provides us with the meaning to all our interactions with the world, as filtered through your beliefs and habits. It communicates through feelings, emotions, imagination, sensations, and dreams.

Is hypnosis similar to meditation?

I have found the best way to explain is this: The intention of meditation is to be still and let all thoughts come by and pass until you get to a state of nothingness and/or zen state. On the other hand, going into hypnosis is to relax the mind and body enough to reach a level that the subconscious mind and bring forth information, feelings, behavior or habit(s) that need a shift or change for the better.

There are specialized ways to make that happen. By continuously being in charge of your own thoughts through directing your focus and using visualization, you can influence what programs the subconscious mind constantly runs.

Education – Empathy – Experience – Equality.

Education – educate yourself by asking detailed questions on social and cultural background of your clients. Knowing something about their culture, tradition or even religion may be of help in why they do what they do. This helps not to step boundaries.

Empathy – having the ability to understand and share certain feelings can be essential to recognizing humility within yourself and others.

Experience – this validates education and authority. What does it feel like to have nothing materialistically, of physically challenged, be different, feel outsider or behavior that is not known to you.

Equality – being aware and accepting that you may have different talents, skills, and beliefs, but we are all human.

Another issue is the on-the-job self-care.

Over the course of our relationships with clients, they may confront, blame, challenge, yell, leave, or fall in love with us. They may remind us of somebody we've known from our past.

Not only do you need to be centered and clear in your responses when this type of transference or counter-transference occurs, but after the client leaves your office, you also need to know how to take care of yourself. We can't expect our clients to make it better for us. We are responsible for the feelings that arise in us after a difficult client interaction.

How to Change Your Life

If you want to affect change in your life at a core level then you will have to work on yourself. We know a heart surgeon does not have to undergo heart surgery to perform surgery on a patient, yet experiencing hypnosis for yourself is essential to your practice so you can comfortably and with no hesitation explain the process and feeling your clients will experience – there is no loss of control, but being more in control.

Be honest – Do the Best YOU can – Treat others with more respect.

This is the power of positive affirmation with proven result. Success feeds success!

We all know words can make or break us. Negative words like "try", "should", "maybe" will not allow your client to achieve results they desire.

Hypnotherapy is about pictures in the subconscious mind and hot to make the sights, sounds, colors, feelings and results of the special pictures created by them be more profound with unlimited significance and power.

Visualization can be profound.

Working with visualization is an easy way to paint a picture in your client's mind. Ask your client to close their eyes and pretend they can see a blackboard with the numbers one to ten written across the top.

Then ask them to pretend they are erasing the number ten and when it is gone to nod her head and say the words – 'deep sleep'. Then ask them to proceed to erase ach number the same way repeating 'deep sleep' after each number erased. By the time number one is erased, they have automatically allowed themselves enter into a relaxed hypnotic state. You can let them know that by using this technique, they can erase numbers whenever they experience discomfort, anxiety, fear, tension or to erase a habit they no longer wish to keep.

Liza's '33 Days' New Habit Forming Theory:

You may have heard the phrase "It takes 21 days to form a habit." My philosophy is that it takes '33 consecutive days of repeating the same thing over and over – either good or bad, to change and form a new habit. Are you wondering why 33 instead of 21 days?

We are creatures of habit and function in a society where everything is measured by "time." This means - we know and understand seconds, minutes, hours, days, weeks and months. The most days in a month are 31.

What if … we continue a new routine for over 33 consecutive days, then we have done it for over an entire month and are already into the next month. Most think and feel "If I can do it for over a month, I can do this again for the next 33 days," thus placing the new programming into action for third month.

It is quite simple; instead of coming short in the month (21 days) you have now accomplished something you did not believe imaginable. While your entire thought process was to do something for 33 days continually, the pressure and the discomfort of "possible failure" is lifted …and by the second month, the new habit is formed! Bingo! You've succeeded and conquered the old habit. Saying to yourself: "I did it" - "it worked"! It – is YOU.

Now that you know the key to healing is within, I wish you all the success and joy in life.

Evoke your Passion (what was)
Embrace Your Femininity (what is)
Evolve Spiritually (what is to be)
Live Victoriously – YOU MATTER

Liza Boubari, CCHt, CSMc
www.HealWithin.com
Lizab@healwithin.com
(818) 551-1501